YOU CAN
QUILT!

BUILDING
SKILLS FOR
BEGINNERS

LEILA
GARDUNIA
&
MARLENE
ODDIE

American Quilter's Society

PO Box 3290 • Paducah, KY 42002-3290
Fax 270-898-1173 • e-mail: orders@AQSquilt.com

Located in Paducah, Kentucky, the American Quilter's Society (AQS) is dedicated to promoting the accomplishments of today's quilters. Through its publications and events, AQS strives to honor today's quiltmakers and their work and to inspire future creativity and innovation in quiltmaking.

EXECUTIVE BOOK EDITOR: KIMBERLY HOLLAND TETREV
SENIOR EDITOR: LINDA BAXTER LASCO
COPY EDITOR: ADRIANA FITCH
GRAPHIC DESIGN: ELAINE WILSON
COVER DESIGN: MICHAEL BUCKINGHAM
PHOTOGRAPHY: CHARLES R. LYNCH

Additional copies of this book may be ordered from the American Quilter's Society, PO Box 3290, Paducah, KY 42002-3290, or online at www.AmericanQuilter.com.

LIBRARY OF CONGRESS CATALOGING-IN-PUBLICATION DATA

Gardunia, Leila.
  You can quilt! : building skills for beginners / by Leila Gardunia and Marlene Oddie.
    pages cm
  Includes bibliographical references and index.
  ISBN 978-1-60460-183-1 (alk. paper)
  1. Quilting. I. Oddie, Marlene. II. Title.
  TT835.G33167 2015
  746.46--dc23
                            2015009446

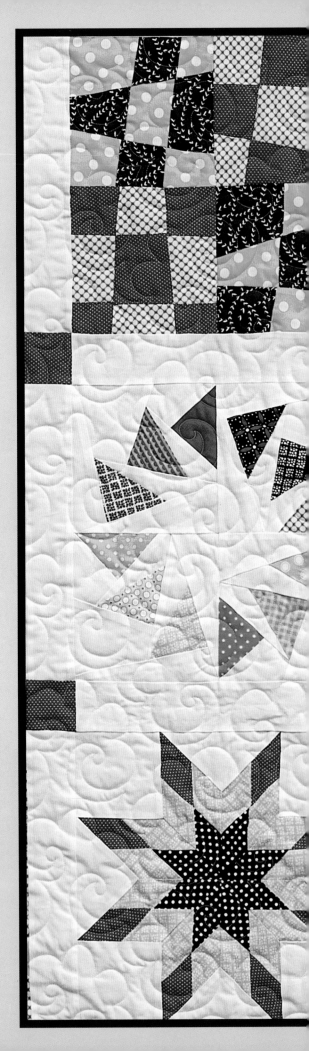

TITLE PAGE: CIRCLE OF GEESE PILLOW, detail. Full pillow shown in Gallery on CD. Block designed by Beth Maddocks, City, State.

RIGHT: YOU CAN DO IT! SKILL BUILDER QUILT, detail. Full quilt shown on page 4.

YOU CAN DO IT! SKILL BUILDER QUILT, 98" x 98".
Pieced by Leila Gardunia and quilted by Marlene Oddie.

Contents

ROSIE's BOMb, 88" x 100".
Designed, pieced, and quilted by Marlene Oddie.

Introduction

In 1943, Constance Bowman and Clara Marie Allen, both school teachers, announced they wanted to support the war effort by working in a bomber factory during their summer vacation. Their friends laughed and said they couldn't. Constance and Clara Marie insisted they could, even though they weren't sure. Their job applications were quickly processed and they went to work building B-24s.

It was very hard work. Exhausted, grimy, and aching, Constance and Clara Marie did their very best. The results weren't always perfect; Constance joked that she could tell which B-24 she had helped to build by the safety belt holders she had riveted on unevenly. Like other real-life Rosie the Riveters, they worked diligently, learned new skills, and were justly proud of their accomplishments.

They discovered they could do it!

As quilters, we are not asked to build bombers but we can push our boundaries and learn skills we thought were far beyond us. The only thing stopping us is fear—the fear of frustration and failure. That little voice in our heads laughs and says, "You can't do it!" Well, it is time to take a deep breath and respond, "I can do it! I can learn to piece a perfect quarter-square triangle! I can learn to sew curves and to foundation paper piece! I can quilt"

This is what *You Can Quilt! Building Skills For Beginners* is all about. It is about empowering you and helping you reach your full potential as a quilter. Each section in this book is dedicated to learning a specific skill. Clear and detailed instructions will guide you throughout. The first block project in each chapter will be fairly simple. The next is moderate in difficulty and the last, challenging. Practice the new skill first on a simple block and, by the end of the chapter, you will be confident you can make any block with that skill, no matter its difficulty.

For your convenience, included with this book is a CD that contains the full-size templates and foundations needed to make some of the blocks. Simply insert the CD into a computer and print the copies you need—no wasting time tracing or copying them.

Our goal is to teach you the skills needed to make the quilts of your dreams. Don't settle for simple and safe if you want to create curved and complex quilts. You can sew the B-24s of quilts! The way might be littered with crooked seams and pricked fingers, but you can do it!

When the 36 skill-building blocks in this book are completed, they can be sewn together to make a You Can Do It! Skill Builder king-size quilt. We would love to see yours. To share pictures of your progress or a finished quilt, upload them to our Flickr group page at: http://www.flickr.com/groups/wecandoitskillbuildersampler/.

Share what you have made and cheer other people along on their journey.

Together, We Can Do It!

You Can Do It!
Skill Builder Quilt Project

Fabrics and Supplies

Listed below are the materials needed to complete the quilt. Before you start, collect a stash of colors and prints that will blend and contrast well. The quantity of fabric needed to make each 12½" x 12½" block is small. At the beginning of each project, choose fabrics from this collection and cut the amount needed to make the block. Use a few fabrics or use many. It is your choice.

Fabric

Fat quarters or half-yard cuts are perfect for this project if you like a scrappy look. If you want a more unified look, one or two yards of each fabric would be more appropriate.

Small to medium prints and solids will be the best choice for most of the blocks, but there will be a few places for large-scale prints to shine, so don't rule them out.

You may choose to have a single fabric for the background of the entire quilt or use different fabrics for the backgrounds of individual blocks. If you use a single background fabric, be sure the other fabrics will stand out well against it and provide sufficient contrast.

Quilt block fabrics

For the same background for each block:

Background	4½ yards
Assorted prints and solids	9 yards

For a different background for each block:

Assorted prints and solids	13 yards

Finishing fabrics

Sashing and inner border	2½ yards
Outer border and cornerstones	2⅞ yards
Binding	⅞ yard
Backing	3 yards of 108" wide

Or 9 yards of standard-width fabric cut into 3 three-yard pieces. Remove the selvages and join along the trimmed edges.

Batting	106" x 106"

Tip

Cutting the borders along the length of the fabric helps keep them square and even but leaves a lot of leftover fabric. Reserve the width of your borders by the entire length of fabric (LOF) from your selected border fabric and use the remaining fabric in the quilt blocks. See page 131 for the cutting measurements for the inner and outer borders.

Supplies

- Sewing machine with both zigzag and straight stitches
- Quality thread that blends with the fabric. White, beige, or gray are good choices.
- Scissors
- Pins
- Seam ripper
- Hand needle
- Cutting mat
- Rotary cutter and extra blades
- Rulers
  Required
    24" x 6" and 12½" x 12½"
  Recommended
    12" x 6" for smaller cuts
    6½" x 6½" and 4½" x 4½" for mid-block trimming
    Add-a-Quarter™ ruler for foundation paper piecing
    Perfect Piecer™ for marking ¼" seam allowance intersections
- Iron and ironing surface
- Freezer paper for appliqué
- Lightweight double-sided interfacing
- Cardstock or clear template plastic
- Marking pens, pencils, or chalk— 1 permanent and 1 removable
- Computer, printer, and the enclosed CD for printing templates and foundations
- Regular copy paper or specialty foundation paper
- Optional
  Quarter-inch presser foot
  Compass
  Digital camera to document progress and to experiment with placement and color

Choosing Fabric

There is nothing more exciting or challenging than choosing fabric for a project. It gets the creative juices flowing; the possibilities are endless and exciting. But with endless possibilities, the choices can seem overwhelming. When choosing fabric for any project, here are a few things to keep in mind.

Type and Quality of Fabric

We recommend using 100% quilting cottons for this quilt. These are easy to cut and sew; they wear well. Poor quality or vintage fabric can be prone to colors running, shrinkage, or shredding. Don't skimp on fabric. It's not worth the risk.

Colors

Choose colors that you love! You may want to make a monochromatic quilt or one with all the colors of the rainbow. If you aren't sure what colors look good together, browse online color-palette sites like www.design-seeds.com for ideas or use a color wheel to choose colors that work well together (Fig. 1, page 10). A local quilt shop can help you select fabrics based on your ideas. There are several ways to combine colors that make for good design. Most importantly, though, is to be true to what you love. You are not going to want to sew with fabrics you don't like.

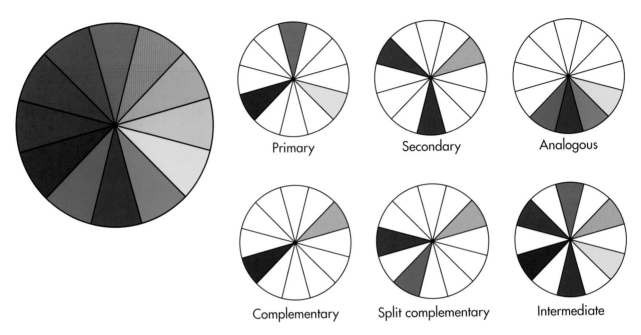

Fig. 1

Value

Once you have an idea of what colors you want to use, be sure to pick different values of them. For example, if you are using blues, be sure to pick light, medium, and dark values of blue. If all of the fabric is the same value, the patchwork design won't stand out and the quilt will look flat and lifeless.

If you can't tell if the fabrics are different in value, take a picture of them and edit it to a black and white photo or use a copy machine to make a black and white copy of them. If there is a difference in value, you should be able to easily tell the grays apart (Fig. 2).

Finished vs. Unfinished Dimensions

For single pieces, the *unfinished* size is the cut size. The *finished* size is how the piece measures after it has been attached on all sides to another block or unit.

Each block is trimmed to measure 12½" x 12½". This is the *unfinished* size of the block. When joined with other blocks with a ¼" seam allowance, you lose ¼" on all sides. The finished size is 12" x 12".

Fig. 2

Skill Builder Set 1
Learning the Basics

Rail Fence

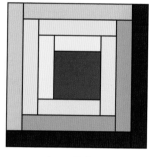

Log Cabin

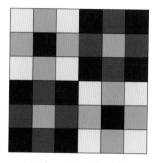

Value Nine-Patch

Are you ready to begin building skills? This Skill Builder set will cover the essentials of cutting, sewing accurate ¼" seams, and pressing. This may seem too basic, but if the cutting and sewing aren't accurate, the points in the block won't match and the quilt blocks will end up being the wrong size. We will also study how color and value placement affects the overall look of a block and introduce strip and chain piecing.

Cutting

When cutting pieces for a quilt, cut along the grain of the fabric—the vertical or horizontal directions the threads are woven. If you cut diagonally across the grain, it is called cutting on the bias (Fig. 1–1). There are times when bias cuts are appropriate, but in general, it is best to cut with the grain of the fabric to avoid the stretching that occurs along bias-cut edges.

Right-handed vs. Left-handed Rotary Cutting

For right-handed cutting, a ruler specifically designed for rotary cutting is held in place with the left hand and the cut is made along the right edge of the ruler with the rotary cutter. Successive cuts are made from left to right across the fabric. For left-handed cutting, the ruler is held in place with the right hand and the cut is made along the

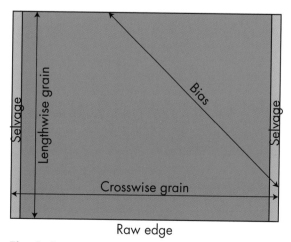

Fig. 1–1

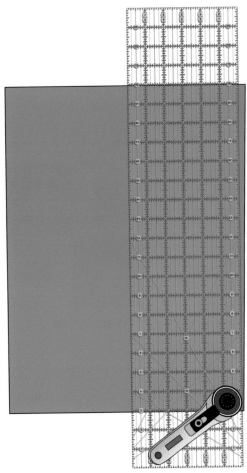

Fig. 1–2

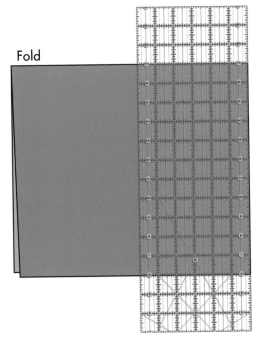

Fold

Fig. 1–3

left edge of the ruler. Successive cuts are made from right to left across the fabric.

Note: The photos all show the position of the ruler on the fabric for right-handed cutting.

The first step when cutting fabric is to square the edges. Squaring means to trim a raw edge so it is perfectly straight. To trim a small piece of fabric, simply place the ruler about ⅛" from the uneven edge, align the ruler with the straight-of-grain and trim it with a rotary cutter (Fig. 1–2).

If squaring a larger piece of fabric, fold it in half along the grain of the fabric. Place the fold parallel with any line that runs the width of the ruler (Fig. 1–3). If the fold is not even along the width of the ruler, the strip will not be straight when it is unfolded.

To cut with a ruler and rotary cutter, firmly place one hand flat on the ruler with at least one finger on the opposite side of the ruler from where you are cutting to hold it steady. Trim along the edge of the ruler with the rotary cutter while keeping your fingers away from the blade. Start cutting close to your body and guide the cutter away from you. The fabric is now squared up.

If not all of the fabric was cut on the first pass, you may need to use more pressure on the rotary cutter or the blade may be dull. Nothing is more frustrating than a dull blade. Replacement blades can be expensive, but being able to cut cleanly and accurately is worth the price.

To square an especially large piece of fabric, like a 108" wide backing, make a small cut on the selvage and tear the width of the fabric to the opposite selvage. This will square the piece to the fabric's grain. You may want to trim it further if tearing the fabric altered the shape of the threads, but at least it is truly squared to the grain.

Now that you have squared the fabric, imagine the instructions ask you to cut a 2½" strip. To do so, align the 2½" mark on the ruler with the trimmed edge of the fabric (Fig. 1–4). The fabric under the ruler will be protected from the cutter going awry. Hold the ruler down firmly and cut a 2½" strip.

If the instructions go on to ask you to cut 2½" x 2½" squares from the 2½" strips (Fig. 1–5), you would:
- Square up the end of the strip.
- Align the top edge of the strip with any inch line on the ruler that extends across the ruler's width.
- Line up the short edge of the fabric with the 2½" mark.
- Cut along the edge of the ruler.

Sewing ¼" Seams

Unless otherwise specified, all seams are sewn ¼" from the fabric edges and with the fabrics placed right sides together. Taking time now to perfect a ¼" seam will ensure the blocks are the correct size. There are several ways to consistently sew a ¼" seam.

Mark the ¼" Spot

To sew accurate ¼" seams, take a scrap of fabric and sew ¼" away from its edge. Most of the time, ¼" is just shy of the edge of a regular sewing foot.

Line up the edge of the fabric with the edge of the ruler. The seam's stitches should be on the ¼" line (Fig. 1–6, page 14). Note whether the seam is a perfect ¼" or a bit too small or too large.

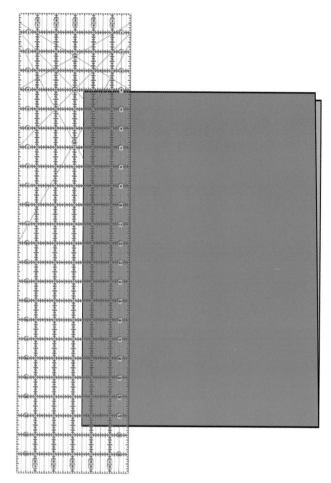

Fig. 1–4

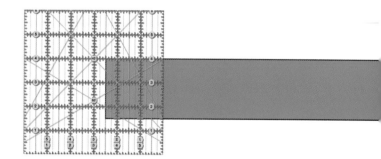

Fig. 1–5

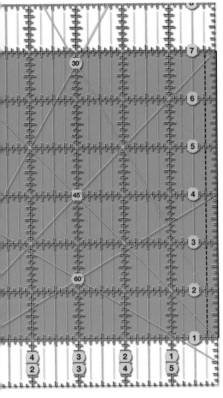

Fig. 1–6

Fig. 1–7

If sewing with the edge of the sewing machine foot did not make a perfect ¼" seam, place a ruler under the foot of the sewing machine and gently lower the needle onto the ¼" mark. Place a sticky note or a piece of masking tape on the bed of the sewing machine along the edge of the ruler (Fig. 1–7). This is the ¼" mark.

Place the fabric edge against the left edge of the tape or sticky note—not on it. Sew another ¼" seam and measure it with a ruler. Is it ¼"?

If not, try again until you figure out where the machine's ¼" sweet spot is. You can do it! Once you have found the perfect ¼" spot, keep a piece of tape on the sewing machine to mark it and ensure consistent seams.

Quarter-Inch Foot

Another option is to invest in a quarter-inch foot. There is a variety of styles available. Some have a piece of metal along the foot's edge that you can use to guide the fabric. Some are designed so that the edge of the foot is exactly ¼" from the center position of the needle. The style depends on the make of your machine. A generic quarter-inch foot that fits many different machines is also available.

Regardless of the design, any quarter-inch foot makes sewing a consistent ¼" seam much easier. However, it is always a good idea to make a test seam and measure your seam allowance to make sure it is exactly ¼" from the line of stitches to the edge of the fabric.

Quarter-Inch Stitch Setting

Some of the newer sewing machines have a ¼" stitch setting that adjusts the needle position so that the edge of a standard sewing foot is truly ¼". Check your sewing machine manual to see if you have such a stitch. Sometimes it is marked with a P for piecing 6.5mm from the edge of the foot. Test the ¼" seam as described earlier.

Pressing

After sewing a seam, the next step is to press it. For best results, set the seam by pressing it with an iron while both fabrics are

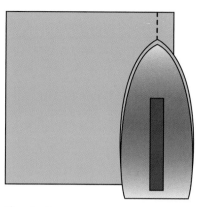

Fig. 1–8a

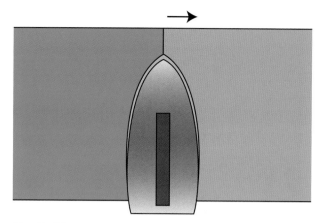

Fig. 1–8b

still right sides together (Fig. 1–8a). Setting the seam will not be specified in all of the block instructions, but it is expected. Be sure to press the fabric and not iron it. Ironing involves pressure and a back-and-forth movement, like ironing a shirt. This type of pressure and movement can cause distortion in a quilt block. Pressing, on the other hand, is simply putting the iron on the fabric with the absolute minimum of movement.

The next step is to open the fabrics and gently press the seam allowance to one side. A general rule is to press toward the darker fabric or whichever way will reduce the bulk of the seams in future piecing (Fig. 1–8b). In this book, each piecing diagram will specify with an arrow which direction to press the seam allowance.

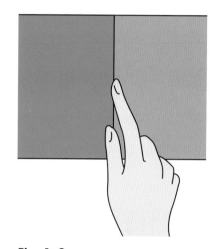

Fig. 1–9a

Examine the seam to make sure all of the fabric was pressed away from the stitching. If there are little flaps of fabric that aren't pressed to the side, the overall size of the block will be affected.

Some quilters choose to finger press or use a wallpaper seam roller to press seams. To do this, hold the fabric firmly with one hand and use the underside of a fingernail from your other hand or a seam roller to press the seam open (Figs. 1–9a and b). This can minimize the effect heat can have in distorting the fabric, especially when dealing with bias seams.

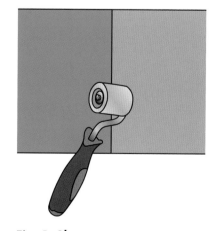

Fig. 1–9b

Now that cutting, sewing, and pressing have been reviewed, you are ready to tackle the first block!

Rail Fence Block

T his simple yet striking block is perfect for practicing cutting strips of fabric and sewing ¼" seams accurately. We will use strip piecing— sewing strips together and then cutting them into smaller units to speed construction.

Fabric

Choose 3 fabrics (A, B, and C) with different values (light to dark).

Cutting

(1) 2½" x at least 26" strip of each fabric

Construction

Sew the A and B strips right sides together with a ¼" seam. Press the seam. Sew the C strip to the right of the B strip (Fig. 1–10). Set the seams and then press them to the side. When pressing long strips, press in small sections along the width of the fabric. Ironing the length of the fabric can distort it.

Measure the middle strip (Fig. 1–11). It should be exactly 2" wide. If not, measure ¼" from the needle to the right edge of the fabric and try again. If the middle strip is still less than 2" wide, try sewing a scant ¼" seam. A scant ¼" seam is one that is just a thread or two smaller than a ¼" seam and will often give the desired results.

Once you have sewn and pressed the strips, square the end of the strip (Fig. 1–12). Subcut (4) 6½" x 6½" squares (Fig. 1–13).

Assembly

Decide which fabric you want in the middle of your block and lay out the squares (Fig. 1–14). Sew 2 squares together and press in the direction of the arrow (Fig. 1–15). Repeat for the 2 remaining squares (Fig. 1–16). Place the sets of squares right sides together and align the center seams. Since the seams are pressed in opposite directions, the pieces should nest together. Pin the center seam and along the edges as needed. Sew the sets together and press in the direction of the arrow (Fig. 1–17).

You did it! The block should measure 12½" x 12½" square.

Fig. 1–10

Fig. 1–11

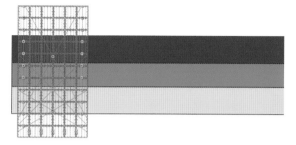

Fig. 1–12

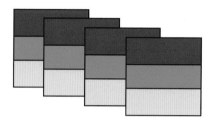

Fig. 1–13

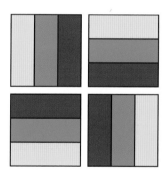

Fig. 1–14

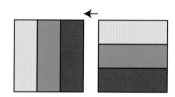

Fig. 1–15

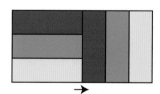

Fig. 1–16

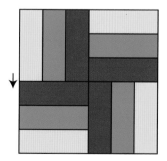

Fig. 1–17

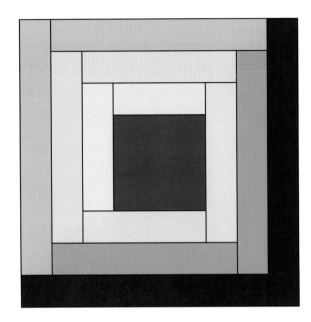

Cutting

Fabric A	3½" x 3½" square
Fabric B	2" x 3½" strip 2" x 5" strip
Fabric C	2" x 5" strip 2" x 6½" strip
Fabric D	2" x 6½" strip 2" x 8" strip
Fabric E	2" x 8" strip 2" x 9½" strip
Fabric F	2" x 9½" strip 2" x 11" strip
Fabric G	2" x 11" strip 2" x 12½" strip

Log Cabin Block

Log Cabin blocks are one of the oldest and most beloved patchwork blocks. The center square represents the hearth of the home. The light-colored logs are the sun shining on the log walls and the dark logs are the shadows. Depending on the arrangement of light and dark fabrics and the layout of blocks, many wonderful designs can be made with this simple block.

This block will provide practice for cutting strips of different lengths. Check the size of the block after each round of logs is added to ensure you are sewing a true ¼" seam. This will allow you to immediately recognize if the seams are off.

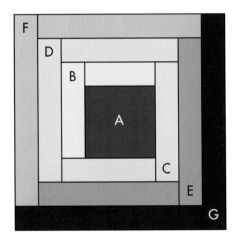

Fig. 1–18

Fabric

Use 2" strips of various fabrics to make this block. You may want to make one side all lights and the other side all darks. You can also choose to make alternate light and dark rings of fabric.

Construction

Lay out the fabric strips to form the block (Fig 1–18). Match the edges of the Fabric A square and the 2" x 3½" Fabric B strip and sew them together. Set the seam and press toward the Fabric B strip (Fig. 1–19). Match the edges of the Fabric AB unit and the 2" x 5" Fabric B strip and sew them together. Set the seam and press toward the longer Fabric B strip (Fig. 1–20).

Referring to Fig. 1–21, add each strip (log) in numerical order and press toward the outside of the block. After the first round of logs, the block should measure 6½" x 6½" square. Measure the block and adjust the seam allowance if necessary. After the second round, the block should measure 9½" x 9½" square. With the third and final round of logs, it should measure 12½" x 12½" square. You did it!

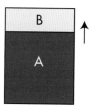

Fig. 1–19

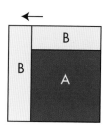

Fig. 1–20

> ## Tip
>
> Remember to trim the thread tails from the end of the seams. This keeps the blocks tidy. Trimming will also help to keep darker threads from showing through light fabrics after the quilt is finished.

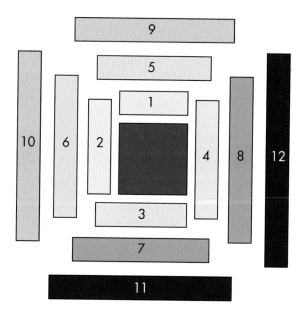

Fig. 1–21

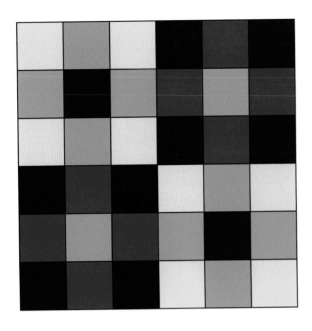

the lights and darks for the secondary pattern in this block to work.

Cutting

Dark 1	(2) 2½" x 11" strips
	(1) 2½" x 6" strip
Dark 2	(2) 2½" x 6" strips
	(1) 2½" x 11" strip
Light 1	(2) 2½" x 11" strips
Light 2	(3) 2½" x 6" strips
	(1) 2½" x 11" strip

Value Nine-Patch Block

The Nine-Patch block is popular, versatile, and excellent for learning how the placement of different color values can create a secondary pattern. Without the differences in values, this block would simply be a 36-Patch block.

With the deliberate placement of light and dark colors, a four-patch pattern is visible. For a more pronounced look, use two colors of the same value for the lights and two colors of the same value for the darks. For example, a dark blue with white polka dots and a dark blue with flowers with a light yellow batik and a light yellow stripe.

Fabric

Choose 2 fabrics that are very dark in value and 2 that are very light. Take a picture of some dark and light fabrics you want to use and look at the picture in black and white to help you choose. There needs to be a significant value difference in

Construction

Sew (3) 11" dark strips together—Dark 1, Dark 2, and Dark 1. Press the seam allowance toward the center (Fig. 1–22). Sew (3) 11" light strips together—Light 1, Light 2, and Light 1. Press seam allowances away from the center (Fig. 1–23). Sew (3) 6" strips together—Dark 2, Light 2, and Dark 2 (Fig. 1–24). Sew the remaining (3) 6" strips together—Light 2, Dark 1, and Light 2. Press toward the dark fabrics (Fig. 1–25).

Square-up the end of each strip-set and cut into 2½" units as shown (Fig. 1-26).

Lay out the units to form the block (Fig. 1–27). Place 2 units right sides together, pin the seams, and sew them together (Fig. 1–28). Without cutting the threads, sew the next 2 units right sides together (Fig. 1–29), and continue adding units, without cutting the thread, until all of them are sewn together in sets of 3, each one making a nine-patch unit (Fig. 1–29). Press the seam allowances in opposite directions to enable the units to nest together (Fig. 1–30).

Dark Dark Dark
1   2   1

Fig. 1–22

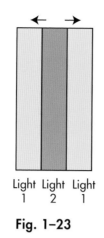

Light Light Light
1   2   1

Fig. 1–23

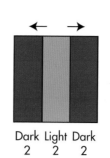

Dark Light Dark
2   2   2

Fig. 1–24

Light Dark Light
2   2   2

Fig. 1–25

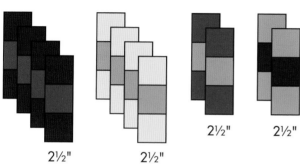

2½"   2½"   2½"   2½"

Fig. 1–26

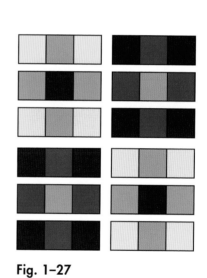

Fig. 1–27

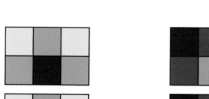

Make 2

Fig. 1–28

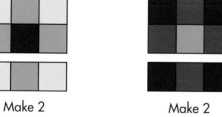

Make 2

Fig. 1–29

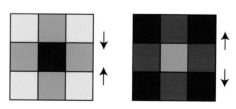

Fig. 1–30

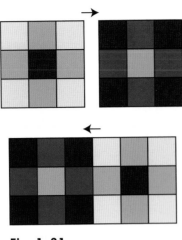

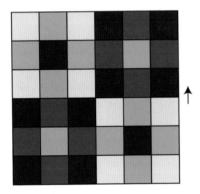

Fig. 1–31

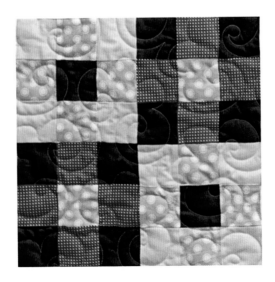

Fig. 1–32

This method of sewing is called chain piecing and will save both time and thread. Use this technique whenever possible. When you have finished sewing all 4 nine-patch units, remove them from the sewing machine and cut them apart. Press the seam allowances toward the darker units.

Assembly

Lay out the 4 nine-patch units to form a block and sew 2 units together. Pay special attention to nesting the seams. Sew the remaining 2 units together. Press the seams toward the dark units (Fig. 1–31). Pin the 2 halves of the block together starting at the center and work outward to ensure the corners are aligned. Sew them together and press (Fig. 1–32).

You did it! The block should measure 12½" x 12½" square.

Skill Builder Set 2
Half-Square Triangles

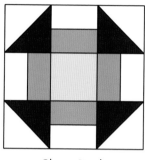

Churn Dash

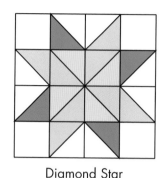

Diamond Star

Arizona

A half-square triangle (HST) is one of the most common and versatile units in quilting (Fig. 2–1). It is simply a square divided in half diagonally with a different fabric in each half. It wouldn't seem that such a unit would pose a problem to piece, but they can be challenging. The diagonal seam needs to be accurately straight in order for the unit to be perfectly square; that can take some practice.

Fig. 2–1

The most intuitive method for making half-square triangles, simply cutting two squares in half diagonally and sewing the different halves back together, is not necessarily the best. Diagonal or bias cuts are prone to distortion while being handled and sewn together. We will show you how to sew seams diagonally on a square to prevent the pieces from stretching and a quick way to make eight half-square triangles at once. You will soon feel confident to tackle any block that uses half-square triangles.

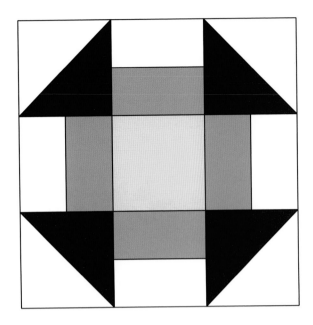

Fabric

Choose 4 contrasting colors (Fig. 2–2).

Cutting

Fabric A	2½" x 19" strip
	4⅞" x 4⅞" square
	5" x 5" square
Fabric B	4½" x 4½" square
Fabric C	2½" x 19" strip
Fabric D	4⅞" x 4⅞" square
	5" x 5" square

Churn Dash Block

This simple block is perfect for practicing half-square triangles. Some quilters cut the fabric so that the triangles are precisely the size needed. This is the easiest method, but it is hard to make them come out exactly square. Others cut the fabric slightly oversized and then trim the unit to the correct size. Trimming takes more time, but the resulting perfectly square units are so easy to work with that it is worth the extra effort. We will use both methods in this block. See which method you prefer.

Strip-Pieced Units

Churn Dash has 4 strip-pieced units on the sides, top, and bottom of the block. Sew the A and C strips together lengthwise (Fig. 2–3). Set the seam and press toward the darker fabric. Square-up the end of the strip-set and cut into (4) 4½" x 4½" squares (Fig. 2-4).

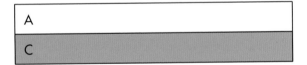

Fig. 2–3

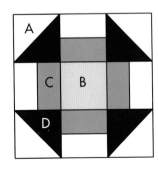

Fig. 2–2

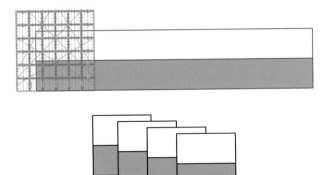

Fig. 2–4

Fig. 2–5

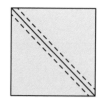

Fig. 2–6

Fig. 2–7

Fig. 2–8

> **Tip**
> Heavily starch the strip fabric before cutting. This will help minimize stretching along the bias edges. Be very careful not to distort the fabric by over handling while making the block or it will not lie flat.

Making Half-Square Triangles (HSTs)

This block also has 4 HSTs. Below are 2 piecing and 2 trimming methods to try. Try these methods and see which you prefer.

Piecing and Trimming Method 1

Draw a diagonal line on the wrong side of the 4⅞" x 4⅞" square of Fabric A (Fig. 2–5). Pair the 4⅞" x 4⅞" squares of Fabrics A and D right sides together. Sew ¼" on either side of the line (Fig. 2–6). Set the seam. Cut on the line (Fig. 2–7) and open the 2 HSTs. Press the seams toward the darker fabric.

The little triangles that stick out at the corners are called dog ears. Trim them off to reduce bulk in the final block (Fig. 2–8). Check that each half-square triangle measures 4½" x 4½" square with the diagonal seam running exactly through the middle of the unit.

If the unit needs additional trimming, find the diagonal 45° line on a ruler and place it on the seam. Make sure the fabric underneath the ruler measures slightly more than 4½" x 4½". Trim the edges that extend beyond the ruler (Fig. 2–9). Rotate the ruler and place the 45° line on the seam again with the previously trimmed edges of the half-square triangle on the 4½" marks. Trim the excess fabric (Fig. 2–10, page 26) to make a perfect 4½" x 4½" HST.

Piecing and Trimming Method 2

Draw a diagonal line across the back of the 5" x 5" square of Fabric A (Fig. 2–5). Pair the 5" x 5" squares of Fabrics A and D right sides together. Sew ¼" on either side of the line (Fig. 2–6). Set the seam and cut on the line (Fig. 2–7).

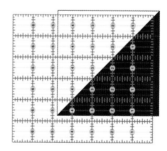

Fig. 2–9

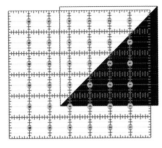

Fig. 2–10

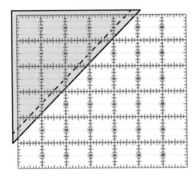

Fig. 2–11

> ## Tip
> Use a small ruler to make trimming easier. A small rotating mat also makes trimming a breeze.

With the half-square triangle still folded in half, match the 4 ½" marks on the ruler with the seam (Fig. 2–11) and trim the excess fabric. Open the triangle unit, press the seam toward the darker fabric, and then trim the dog ears.

Assembly

Lay out the strip-pieced units, HSTs, and the Fabric B square (Fig. 2–12).

To speed up the assembly of a block, use this chain-piecing technique. Begin with the top 2 units on the left and sew them together (Fig. 2–13). Without cutting the thread, sew together the 2 middle left units, and then sew the 2 bottom left units together. Again, without cutting the thread, sew the right units to the previously sewn left units (Fig. 2–14). Cut the threads and press the seams in the direction of the arrows.

Pin and sew the top 2 rows together and then pin and sew the bottom row on the block (Fig. 2–15). Press the rows following the arrows. You can use this method to piece together the units on any block.

The completed Churn Dash block should measure 12½" x 12½". You did it! Sit back and admire the block.

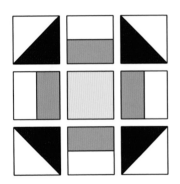

Fig. 2–12

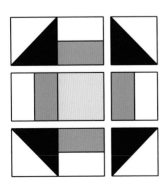

Fig. 2–13

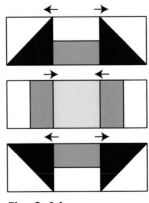

Fig. 2–14

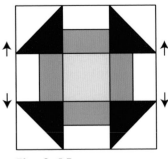

Fig. 2–15

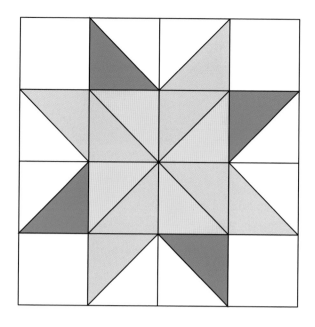

Diamond Star Block

This block is simple yet striking. We are dialing up the difficulty by making smaller half-square triangles. We prefer trimming the half-square triangles to size (see Making Half-Square Triangles on page 25). The measurements for that method are given for this block and throughout the rest of the book. If you are not a fan of trimming, simply cut the squares for the half-square triangles ⅛" smaller than the given measurements.

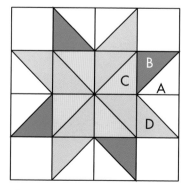

Fig. 2–16

Fabric

Choose 4 contrasting fabrics—3 for the star and 1 for the background (Fig. 2–16).

Cutting

Fabric A	(4) 4" x 4" squares
	(4) 3½" x 3½" squares
Fabric B	(2) 4" x 4" squares
Fabric C	(2) 4" x 4" squares
Fabric D	(4) 4" x 4" squares

Tip

For precise piecing, determine the *finished* size of your HST, then cut your squares ⅞" larger than the finished size. If you wish to make the HST a little larger and then trim to size, cut your squares 1" larger than the finished size. In the Diamond Star block, the HST finished size is 3" x 3".

Construction

Draw a line from corner to corner on the back of the 4 Fabric A squares and on the 2 Fabric C squares. Pair the Fabric A squares right sides together with the 2 Fabric B squares and 2 of the Fabric D squares. Pair the Fabric C squares right sides together with the remaining Fabric D squares.

Chain piece the squares by stitching a ¼" seam on one side of the line for each pair and then sew on the other side of the line. Set the seams,

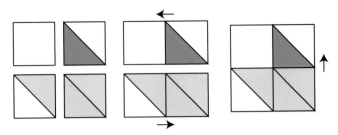

Fig. 2–17

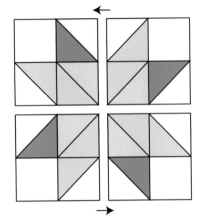

Fig. 2–18a

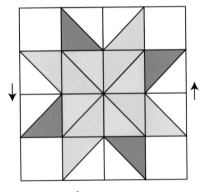

Fig. 2–18b

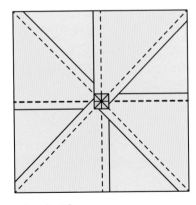

Fig. 2–19

cut the squares on the lines, then press and set the seams. Trim the units to 3½" x 3½" square using one of the trimming methods described on pages 25–26.

Assembly

Lay out 3 half-square triangles sets and a Fabric A square (Fig. 2–17). Sew them together into a four-patch unit and then make 3 more of these. Lay out the 4 four-patch units and sew them together (Figs. 2–18a and b).

In the center of the Diamond Star block are 8 intersecting seams. To minimize the bulk, press the center seam up on one side and down on the other. Gently tease apart the center intersection and fan the seam around. The center seam allowances should form a pinwheel design (Fig. 2–19). You did it! The block should measure 12½" x 12½" square.

Arizona Block

To make this block, we will show you a method to make eight half-square triangles at a time. This is a great time saver for any quilt requiring a lot of half-square triangles.

Fabrics

Choose 2 shades of a color that will contrast well with the background (Fig. 2–20). Play around with the colors. Perhaps you could substitute a fourth color for the rectangles or choose a large-scale fabric and "fussy cut" the inner square (that is, cut the square so a particular design in the fabric is centered in the square).

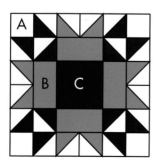

Fig. 2–20

Cutting

Fabric A	(4) 2½" x 2½" squares
	(2) 6" x 6" squares
	(2) 3" x 3" squares
Fabric B	(1) 6" x 6" square
	(4) 2½" x 4½" rectangles
Fabric C	(1) 4½" x 4½" square
	(2) 3" x 3" squares
	(1) 6" x 6" square

Construction

To make 8 half-square triangles at a time, draw a diagonal line both ways on the backs of the 6" x 6" squares of Fabric A (Fig. 2–21). Pair the Fabric A squares right sides together with the 6" x 6" squares of Fabrics B and C. Sew ¼" seams on both sides of the lines (Fig. 2–22). Set the seams. Cut the squares in half vertically and horizontally (Fig. 2–23). Without moving any pieces, cut on the diagonal in both directions along the drawn lines (Fig. 2–24). Press the half-square triangles open and trim them to 2½" x 2½" square, yielding 8 units per set.

Fig. 2–21

Fig. 2–22

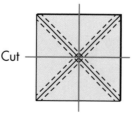

Fig. 2–23

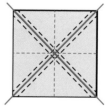

Fig. 2–24

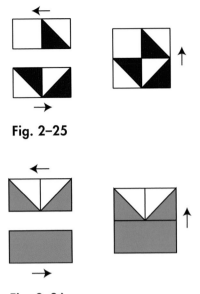

Fig. 2–25

Fig. 2–26

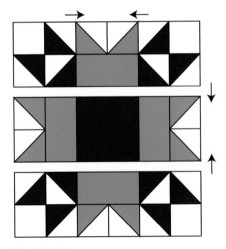

Fig. 2–27

Fig. 2–28

To make the remaining 4 half-square triangles, mark a diagonal line on the backs of the 3" x 3" squares of Fabric A. Pair them right sides together with the 3" x 3" squares of Fabric C. Stitch ¼" from each side of the lines. Set the seams and cut on the lines. Trim each to 2½" x 2½" square. Lay out a four-patch unit with 3 Fabric AC half-square triangles units and a Fabric A 2½" x 2½" squares (Fig. 2–25). Arrange and sew them together. Make (4) four-patch units. Press in the direction of the arrows.

Assembly

Lay out 2 Fabric AB half-square triangles units and 1 Fabric B rectangle (Fig. 2–26). Arrange and sew them together.

Lay out the finished units and the 4½" x 4½" Fabric C square (Fig. 2–27). Sew the units together in rows and then press them (Fig. 2–28). Sew the rows together and press the finished block.

You did it! The block should measure 12½" x 12½" square. If you can make this block, you are able to tackle whatever half-square triangle blocks come your way.

Skill Builder Set 3
Quarter-Square Triangles

Ohio Star

Beacon Light

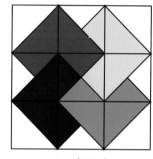

Card Trick

A quarter-square triangle (QST) is simply a square made from four triangles (Fig. 3–1). Many fun designs are possible with the basic quarter-square triangle unit. In this chapter, we will show you a quick-piecing method, how to trim the units to size, and end with a fun quarter-square triangle variation. Let's do it!

Fig. 3–1

Ohio Star Block

Acccording to Jinny Beyer in her book, *The Quilter's Album of Patchwork Patterns*, (Breckling Press, 2009), this classic block was first published in 1862 in *Godey's Lady's Book*. It has had many names but is most commonly known as Ohio Star, the name it was published under in *Capper's Farmer* in 1927. The Ohio Star is an example of how a combination of simple shapes can lead to a striking and enduring quilt block.

Fabric

Choose 2 contrasting colors (Fig. 3–2).

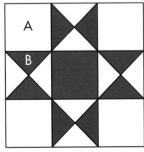

Fig. 3–2

Cutting

Fabric A   (4) 4½" x 4½" squares
(2) 5¼" x 5¼" squares

Fabric B   (2) 5¼" x 5¼" squares
(1) 4½" x 4½" square

Construction

Draw a diagonal line on the wrong side of the 5¼" x 5¼" squares of Fabric A (Fig. 3–3). Pair the A squares right sides together with the 5¼" x 5¼" Fabric B squares. Sew a scant ¼" on both sides of the diagonal lines (Fig. 3–4). Press to set the seam and cut on the diagonal lines (Fig. 3–5). Open the resulting half-square triangles and press toward the darker fabric (Fig. 3–6).

Cut the half-square triangles on the diagonal opposite from the seam (Fig. 3–7). Switch halves with another set (Fig. 3–8), pin to match the center seams making sure the seams nest together. Sew them together. Trim to 4½" x 4½" (Fig. 3–9).

Fig. 3–3

Fig. 3–4

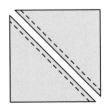

Fig. 3–5

Fig. 3–6

Fig. 3–7

Fig. 3–8

Fig. 3–9

Assembly

Lay out the 4 quarter-square triangles, the (4) 4½" x 4½" Fabric A squares and the 4½" x 4½" Fabric B square (Fig. 3-10).

Sew the pieces into rows (Fig. 3–11). Press the seams in the direction of the arrows. Match the seams and sew each row together (Fig. 3–12). Press.

You did it! The block should measure 12½" x 12½". The next block will use the same techniques but with a more complicated layout.

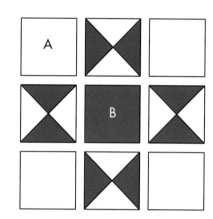
Fig. 3–10

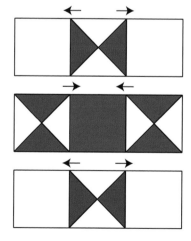
Fig. 3–11

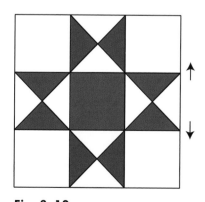
Fig. 3–12

Beacon Light Block

W e will use the same techniques to make quarter-square triangles for this block as we did with the Ohio Star block, however, we will make them slightly larger and trim them to size. When choosing fabrics, you might consider using a large-scale print for the center square.

Fabric

Choose 3 contrasting colors (Fig. 3–13) When choosing fabrics, you might consider using a large-scale print for the center square.

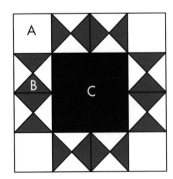

Fig. 3–13

Cutting

Fabric A (4) 3½" x 3½" squares
(4) 4½" x 4½" squares

Fabric B (4) 4½" x 4½" squares

Fabric C (1) (4) 6½" x 6½" square

> ### Tip
> To make precision quarter-square triangles, cut the squares 1¼" larger than the finished unit size (in this case 3" x 3"). If you wish to trim the quarter-square triangles to size, cut the squares 1½" larger than the finished size.

Construction

Make 8 quarter-square triangles with the 4½" x 4½" Fabric A and B squares using the same method illustrated on pages 32–33.

Trim the quarter-square triangles to size by placing the 45° line of the ruler on the diagonal seam line. Make sure the seam intersection at the center of the block is 1¾" from both the top and the right side of the ruler (Fig. 3–14). Trim the top and right sides of the block. Rotate the quarter-square triangle and trim the opposite sides. The middle of the quarter-square triangle should still be at the 1¾" mark. The left and bottom sides of the QST should line up at the 3½" mark (Fig. 3–15). Trim the block to 3½" x 3½".

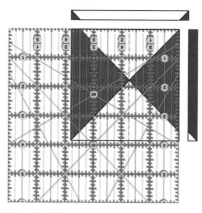

Fig. 3–14

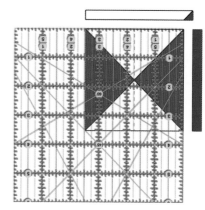

Fig. 3–15

Sew sets of 2 quarter-square triangles together (Fig. 3–16). Make 4 units of 2 quarter-square triangles. Sew the 3½" x 3½" Fabric A squares to both ends of 2 of the quarter-square triangle units (Fig. 3–17). Press in the direction of the arrows.

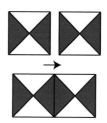

Fig. 3–16

Assembly

Lay out all of the pieces (Fig. 3–18) and sew the double QST units to either side. Press towards the center. Sew on the top and bottom rows. Pin to match seams. You did it! The blocks should measure 12½" x 12½" square

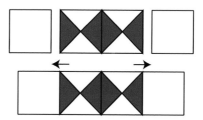

Fig. 3–17

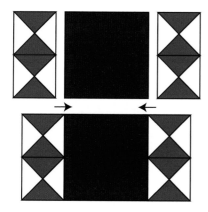

Fig. 3–18a

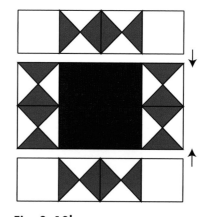

Fig. 3–18b

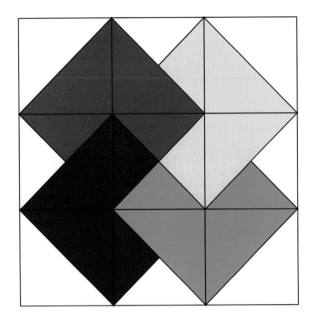

Card Trick Block

This block combines half-square triangles, quarter-square triangles, and a quarter-square triangle variation called a Boston. The way the units work together make this block a fun trick, but use care as you sew; if the fabrics are not placed correctly, the trick won't work.

Fabric

Choose 5 contrasting colors (Fig. 3–19).

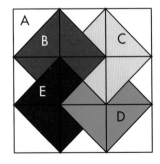

Fig. 3–19

Cutting

Fabric A   (2) 5" x 5" squares cut on the diagonal

(1) 5½" x 5½" square cut on the diagonal both ways

Fabrics B, C, D, and E

(1) 5" x 5" square from each fabric cut on the diagonal

(1) 5½" x 5½" square from each fabric cut on the diagonal both ways

The 4 triangles cut from the 5" x 5" squares are a little larger than the 8 triangles cut from the 5½" x 5½" squares. Two of the smaller triangles from each of Fabrics B, C, D, and E are extra and will not be used in this block but they can be saved to be used in other blocks such as the String block (pages 55–57).

Tip

To help the triangles retain their shape along the bias edges, starch the fabric before cutting. Spray starch lightly, press, and let dry. Repeat.

Construction

Make 4 half-square triangle units each using a triangle cut from the 5" x 5" squares of Fabric A and 1 colored triangle cut from the 5" x 5" square from Fabrics B, C, D and E. These are the larger of the 2 sizes of triangles. Place them right sides together and sew a ¼" seam on the diagonal. Press the seam toward the Fabric A triangle and trim to 4½" x 4½" square (Fig. 3–20).

Lay out the entire block to ensure the colors are placed correctly. Place the half-square triangles in each corner (Fig. 3–21) and then add the small Fabric A triangle between the half-square triangles with the longest side at the edge of the block (Fig. 3–22). Next, add the large colored triangles (Fig. 3–23), and then the small colored triangles (Figs. 3–24 and 3–25).

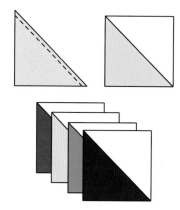

Fig. 3–20

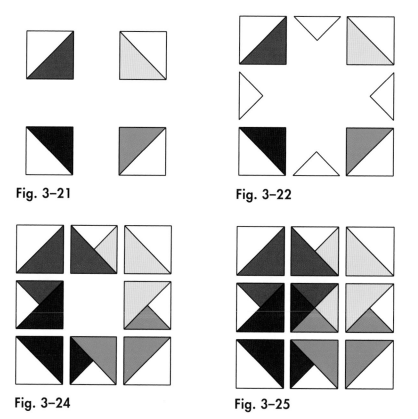

Fig. 3–21   **Fig. 3–22**   **Fig. 3–23**

Fig. 3–24   **Fig. 3–25**

Make a quarter-square triangle using one triangle each of Fabrics B, C, D, and E. Make sure the triangles are placed in the correct sequence (Fig. 3–26). Trim the unit to 4½" x 4½" square. Line up the middle intersection with the 2¼" mark on the ruler while trimming. This quarter-square triangle is center unit of the block.

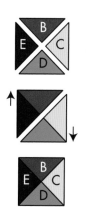

Fig. 3–26

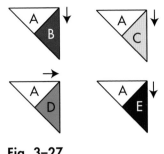

Fig. 3–27

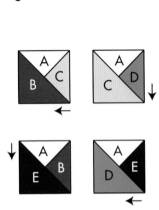

Fig. 3–28

Make 4 Boston units. Start by sewing a smaller Fabric A triangle to the smaller Fabric B, C, D, and E triangles to make half of 4 quarter-square triangles. Press in the direction of the arrows (Fig. 3–27). Sew a larger triangle to each of the partial quarter-square triangle units. Carefully note the fabric placement of each unit (Fig. 3–28) Press. Trim to 4½" x 4½" square. Line up the center of each unit with the 2¼" mark on the ruler and the seam along the diagonal while trimming.

Assembly

Lay out all pieces (Fig. 3–29). Sew into rows and press (Fig. 3–30). Sew the rows together (Fig. 3–31). Keep the middle row on top when you stitch so you can see where the points are for each seam intersection. The outer diagonal seams should nest. Fan the center intersections if desired to reduce bulk. Press firmly.

You did it! The block should measure 12½" x 12½" square.

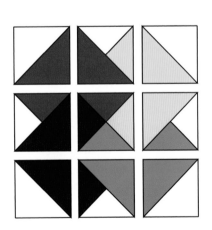

Fig. 3–29

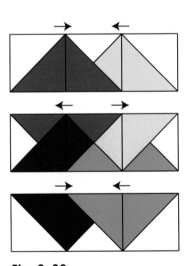

Fig. 3–30

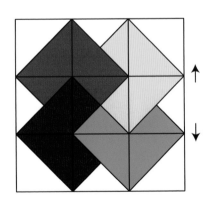

Fig. 3–31

YOU CAN QUILT! Building Skills for Beginners ● Leila Gardunia & Marlene Oddie

Skill Builder Set 4
Flying Geese

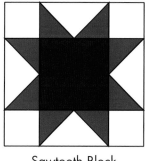

Sawtooth Block

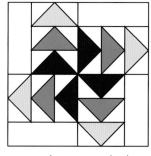

Breaking Out Block

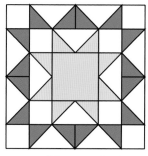

Double Star Block

Flying Geese are a classical shape (Fig. 4–1). In addition to being used within quilt blocks, whole quilts are made completely of flying geese units. The central triangle is called a goose and the two on its sides are the wings. We will explore three different ways to make flying geese units.

Fig. 4–1

Sawtooth Block

The Sawtooth block is another classical favorite. We will use traditional precision cuts to make the flying geese units. Be careful when handling the pieces. They are prone to stretching along the bias cuts. Starch will help stabilize the edges of the triangles. (See the Tip on starching, page 36.)

Fabric

Choose 3 contrasting colors (Fig. 4–2).

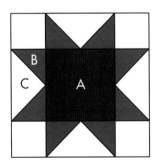

Fig. 4–2

Cutting

Fabric A   (1) 6½" x 6½" square

Fabric B   (4) 3⅞" x 3⅞" squares cut on the diagonal in one direction

Fabric C   (4) 3½" x 3½" squares
(1) 7¼" x 7¼" square cut on the diagonal in both directions

Construction

Place a Fabric B triangle right sides together with one side of a Fabric A triangle. Sew together using a scant ¼" seam (Fig. 4–3). Set the seam. Open and press the seam toward Fabric B (Fig. 4–4). Be sure to lift the iron straight up and down to avoid stretching the bias edge. Repeat for opposite side (Fig. 4–5). Trim off the dog ears.

Check the seam allowance at the top of the goose where the B triangle seams cross. It should measure ¼" from the point of the goose to the edge of the seam (Fig. 4–6). Trim if needed. The flying geese unit should measure 3½" x 6½". Repeat to make 4 flying geese units.

Assembly

Lay out the block pieces (Fig. 4–7). Sew each row together (Fig. 4–8). When you sew a flying geese unit to the other pieces, make sure you sew through the point where the seams intersect at the top of the goose (Fig. 4–9). If you sew below the intersection, the point of the goose will be cut off. Press using figure 4-8 as a guide. Pin at the seams and join rows together (Fig. 4–10). You did it! Press and admire. The block should measure 12½" x 12½" square.

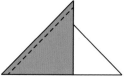

Fig. 4–3

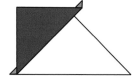

Fig. 4–4

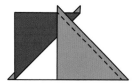

Fig. 4–5

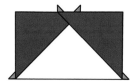

Fig. 4–6

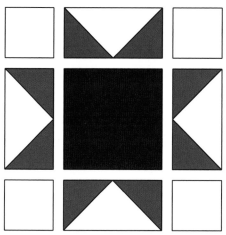

Fig. 4–7

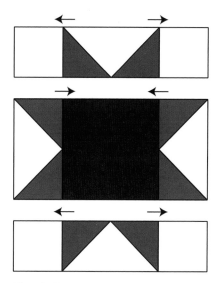

Fig. 4–8

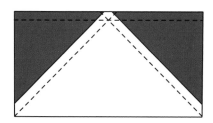

Fig. 4–9

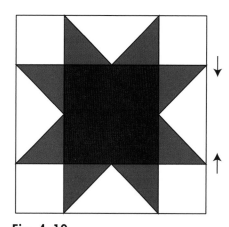

Fig. 4–10

Breaking Out Block

I n this striking block, designed by Jennie Finch, we use a corner-to-corner method of making flying geese. Construction is easy and accurate making this method is especially practical when sewing tiny flying geese units where precision is important.

Fabric

Choose 4 contrasting colors (Fig. 4–11).

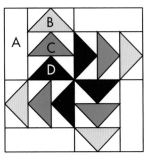

Fig. 4–11

Cutting

Fabric A   (4) 6½" x 2½" rectangles
          (24) 2½" x 2½" squares

Fabrics B, C, and D
          (4) 2½" x 4½" rectangles

Construction

Make 12 flying geese units—4 of each from Fabrics B, C, and D. Draw a diagonal line from corner to corner on the back of each of the 24 Fabric A squares (Fig. 4–12).

Place a 2½" x 2½" Fabric A square, right sides together on one end of a 2½" x 4½" rectangle of Fabric B, C, or D. Match the edges and sew on the line from corner to corner (Fig. 4–13). Trim the outer corner ¼" from the seam (Fig. 4–14). Press the seam toward the goose (Fig. 4–15).

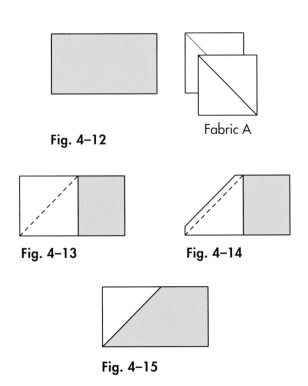

Fig. 4–12

Fabric A

Fig. 4–13

Fig. 4–14

Fig. 4–15

Place a second square on the opposite end of the Fabric B rectangle. Refer to figure 4-16 and make sure the diagonal line faces the correct way. Sew on the line. Trim off the corner and press towards the wing (Fig. 4–17). This is a flying goose! It should measure 2½" x 4½". Repeat to make 12 flying geese units. If needed, trim the units. Make sure to leave a ¼" seam allowance at the tip of the goose and make sure that the 2 fabrics join in a point at the outer corners.

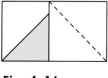

Fig. 4–16

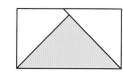

Fig. 4–17

Assembly

Lay out 3 flying geese units, one of each color, and a Fabric A rectangle (Fig. 4–18). Sew the geese together in a column and press in the direction of the arrows (Fig. 4–19). Add the rectangle to the left side (Fig. 4–20). Check the unit to make sure it measures 6½" x 6½" square. Make 4 of these units. Sew together in 2 rows of 2 units each, then sew the rows together (Fig. 4-21).

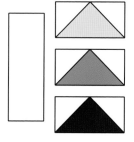

Fig. 4–18

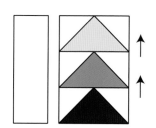

Fig. 4–19

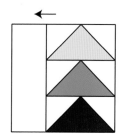

Fig. 4–20

To reduce bulk at the middle of the block, tease the middle seam apart and fan the seam allowances to make a pinwheel as described in Fig. 2–19 on page 28. You did it! The block should measure 12½" x 12½" square.

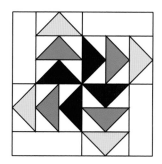

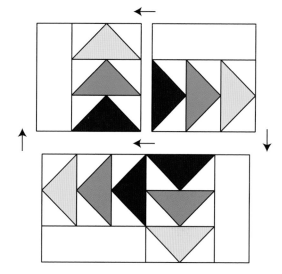

Fig. 4–21

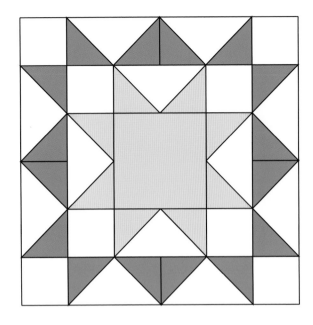

Double Star Block

For this block we introduce the magic method to make the flying geese. When you start sewing, the units look nothing like geese and then, voila! You've made 4 flying geese units at once! Magic!

Fabric

Choose 3 contrasting colors (Fig. 4–22).

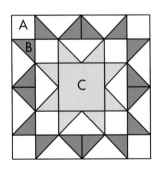

Fig. 4–22

Cutting

Fabric A   (8) 2½" x 2½" squares
              (3) 5¼" x 5¼" squares

Fabric B   (8) 2⅞" x 2⅞" squares

Fabric C   (1) 4½" x 4½" square
              (4) 2⅞" x 2⅞" squares

Construction

Draw a diagonal line on the wrong side of each 2⅞" x 2⅞" square of Fabrics B and C (Fig. 4–23). Pin 2 Fabric B squares on opposite corners of a 5¼" x 5¼" Fabric A square (Fig. 4–24). The squares will overlap in the middle and the drawn lines will run from corner to corner. Stitch a scant ¼" seam on both sides of the line (Fig. 4–25). Press to set the seam. Cut on the diagonal line (Fig. 4–26). Press the seams toward Fabric A (Fig. 4–27). You now have 2 heart shapes!

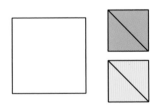

Fig. 4–23

Fig. 4–24

Fig. 4–25

Fig. 4–26

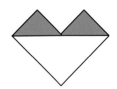

Fig. 4–27

Add a Fabric B square on the remaining corner of each heart-shaped unit (Fig. 4–28). Stitch ¼" on either side of the line (Fig. 4–29). Cut on the diagonal line (Fig. 4–30). Press the seams toward Fabric B (Fig. 4–31). Just like magic, you've made 4 flying geese units! Each unit should measure 2½" x 4½". Repeat these steps with Fabrics A and C to make 8 flying geese.

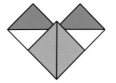

Fig. 4–28

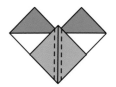

Fig. 4–29

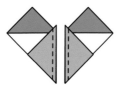

Fig. 4–30

Fig. 4–31

Assembly

Lay out the units for the inner star (Fig. 4–32). Sew together into rows (Fig. 4–33). Press in the direction of the arrows. Join the rows together (Fig. 4–34) and press. To make the outer star units, sew 2 flying geese made with Fabric B together (Fig. 4–35). Make 4 of these units. Press the seams. As they are quite bulky, you may press them open if you like.

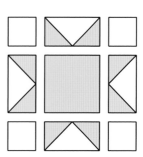

Fig. 4–32

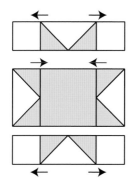

Fig. 4–33

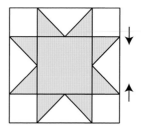

Fig. 4–34

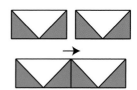

Fig. 4–35

■Flying Geese ■
■Double Star Block ■

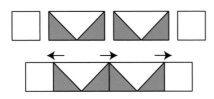

Fig. 4–36

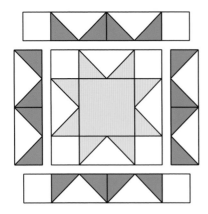

Fig. 4–37

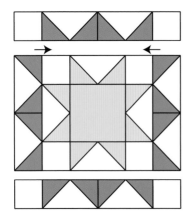

Fig. 4–38

Sew a 2½" x 2½" Fabric A square to each end of 2 of the flying geese units. Press the seams as shown (Fig. 4–36). If you wish to ease the bulk, press the seams open. Lay out the block units (Fig. 4–37). Pin the shorter flying geese units to each side of the inner star at the seams and the flying geese points and then sew them together (Fig. 4–38). Press the seam allowances toward the inner star. Pin and sew the longer flying geese units to the top and bottom of the block (Fig. 4–39). Set and press the seam allowances toward the outer star.

You did it! The block should measure 12½" x 12½" square. This was a challenging block but you did it and now you know a great magic trick.

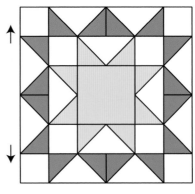

Fig. 4–39

Skill Builder Set 5
Wonky Blocks

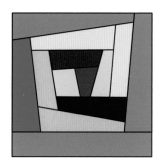

Wonky Log Cabin

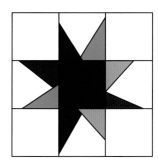

Wonky Star Block

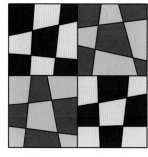

Wonky Nine-Patch

Quilters have been making blocks with odd-sized pieces ever since there were odd-sized scraps, but the current popularization of wonky blocks started with the publication of Gwen Marston's landmark book, *Liberated Quiltmaking*, (AQS, 1996). Gwen showed how to free traditional blocks from exact cutting and piecing requirements. The quilting community embraced her techniques. There are now hundreds of online tutorials for all sorts of wonky and improvisational blocks.

We will show how to make three common wonky blocks each based on a classical blocks—Log Cabin, Sawtooth, and Nine Patch. Have fun making these classic blocks; each will have its own unique personality. We are leaving the world of exact angles and cutting behind but we aren't going to throw out all the rules. The cuts should still be straight and the seams should be ¼". We want the blocks to be fun and free, but not to fall apart. Let's get going!

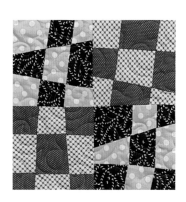

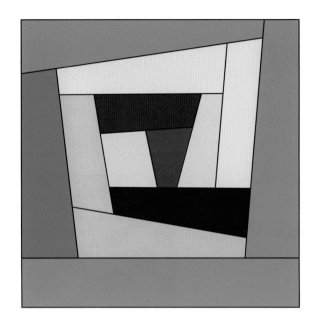

Wonky Log Cabin Block

This is one of Leila's favorite blocks to make. It is so freeing to be able to sew strips, press, cut, and repeat without worrying about exact measuring. It is exciting to see the blocks grow and experiment with different color combinations. Plus, it is a great scrap buster! This block is created by rounds of similar colors but you could make one side of the block one color and the other side another or you could make it completely scrappy.

Fabric

Your choice! Scraps work well.

Cutting

(1) 2" – 4" piece of fabric for the center

Various 2" – 14" lengths x 2" – 4" widths of many fabrics.

Construction

Decide which fabric you would like for the center of the block; it can be any size and shape. The example block uses a trapezoid but feel free to use a square for the center if you prefer. Next choose a strip at least as long as the center piece (Fig. 5–1). With right sides together sew the center and the strip together with a ¼" seam (Fig. 5–2). Press the seam toward the strip.

Trim an adjacent side straight (Fig. 5–3). Sew a second strip of fabric across the straightened side (Fig. 5–4). This block is made in a clockwise direction but you can work counter clockwise or even add a strip to the opposite side. There really are no rules.

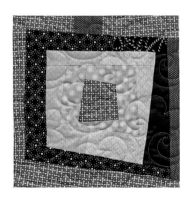

Block Variation

Fig. 5–1

Fig. 5–2

Fig. 5–3

Fig. 5–4

Fig. 5–5a

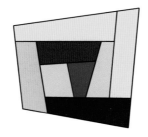

Fig. 5–5b

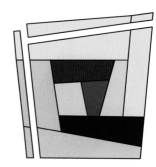

Fig. 5–6

Keep trimming, adding strips to each side, and pressing outward. Trim at a variety of angles (Figs. 5–5a and b). This will add interest and make the wonkiness look intentional, not accidental. You can sew strips together and use these pieced strips as logs (Fig. 5–6). As you add rings to the block, check the size from time to time. When you get near 9"–10", make the last few strips extra wide (Fig. 5–7). This will give you some wiggle room for trimming.

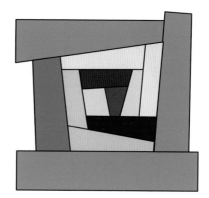

Fig. 5–7

When the block is at least 12½" on each side, trim it to 12½" x 12½" square. A square 12½" ruler comes in handy here. Place it over the block and trim on each side (Fig. 5–8). Play with the angle of the ruler before trimming to see if you like one wonky angle better than another (Fig. 5–9). You did it! The block should measure 12½" x 12½" square.

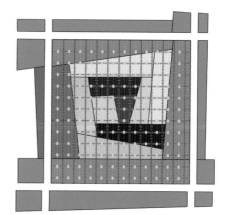

Fig. 5–8

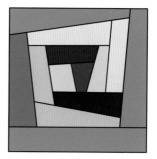

Fig. 5–9

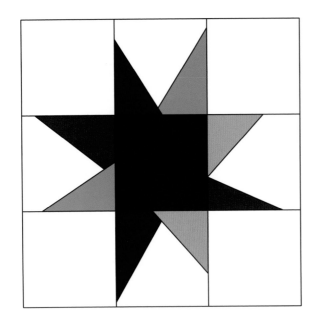

Wonky Star Block

Here's another wonky classic. These stars are so easy and fun to make. Let's get going!

Fabric

Choose 3–5 contrasting fabrics.

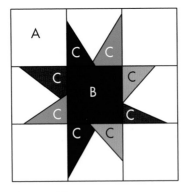

Fig. 5–10

Cutting

Fabric A   (8) 4½" x 4½" squares

Fabric B   (1) 4½" x 4½" square

Fabric C   (4) 5" x 5" squares from 1–3 fabrics

Construction

Cut the 5" x 5" Fabric C squares in half along the diagonal (Fig. 5–11) for the star points. Place a Fabric C triangle right sides together with and on top of a Fabric A square (Fig. 5–12). The triangle piece can be at any angle but when sewn and pressed into place, it needs to cover all of one corner of the Fabric A square (Fig. 5–13a). If it doesn't, the square will end up too small (Fig. 5–13b). To ensure the C triangle will cover the corner of the square completely, place a pin where the seam would be. Flip the triangle down and see if it completely covers the corner of the A square. After a few triangles, you will get a feel for what angles will work.

Sew along the long edge of the triangle with a ¼" seam (Fig. 5–14). Trim off the corner of the Fabric A square (Fig. 5–15). Press the seam allowance toward the triangle (Fig. 5–16). Place a second Fabric C triangle over an adjacent corner of the A square (Fig, 5–17). To add interest, make the angle of this triangle different from the first one. Sew and then trim the Fabric A corner (Fig. 5–18). Press the seam allowance toward Fabric C (Fig. 5–19). Trim the unit to 4½" x 4½" square (Fig. 5–20). Make 4 of these star point units.

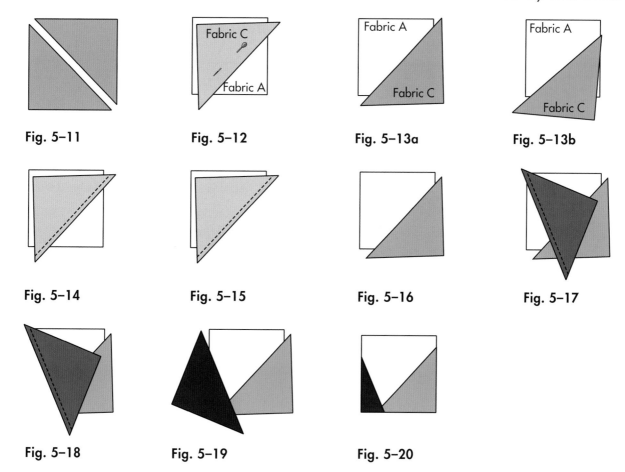

Fig. 5–11   Fig. 5–12   Fig. 5–13a   Fig. 5–13b

Fig. 5–14   Fig. 5–15   Fig. 5–16   Fig. 5–17

Fig. 5–18   Fig. 5–19   Fig. 5–20

Assembly

Lay out the block (Fig. 5–21). Sew the units in 3 rows of 3 units each (Fig. 5–22). Press the seams toward the center and the corner squares. Pin the rows together at the seam intersections and then sew them together (Fig. 5–23). You did it! Make sure the block measures 12½" x 12½" square.

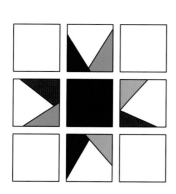

Fig. 5–21

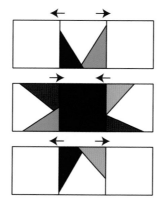

Fig. 5–22

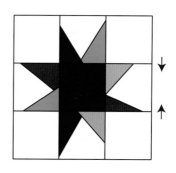

Fig. 5–23

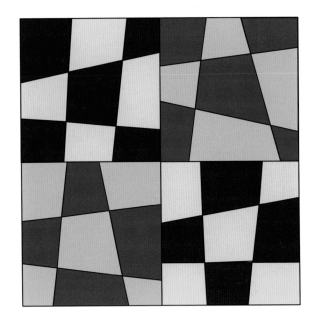

Wonky Nine Patch Block

This is a fun spin on the classic Nine Patch block. Give it a whirl and see how you like it.

Fabric

Choose 4 contrasting colors (Fig. 5–24).

Cutting

Fabrics A, B, C, and D

(1) 8½" x 8½" square of each fabric

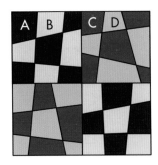

Fig. 5–24

Construction

Choose 2 fabrics and place them face up, one on top of the other. Make 2 angled vertical cuts (Fig. 5–25) at least 2" away from the edges of the fabric squares. Without moving the fabrics, make 2 angled horizontal cuts (Fig. 5–26). Alternate the 2 fabrics so they form 2 nine-patch units (Fig. 5–27a and b). Be careful to keep the fabric pieces in the same places so they will fit together correctly. Sew the pieces together into rows and press in the direction of the arrows (Fig. 5–28a and b). Sew the rows together (Fig. 5–29a and b). The seams will not match exactly; that is okay. Press the seams. Trim the units to 6½" x 6½" squares. Repeat to make 2 more wonky nine-patch units.

Tip

Because the pieces are cut at odd angles, the edges of the rows might not be completely straight. Feel free to trim the edges a bit while still keeping the angle of the piece or simply sew the rows together with a ⅜" seam allowance to compensate for the jagged edges.

Assembly

Arrange the 4 wonky nine-patch units (Fig. 5–30). Sew them together in 2 rows of 2 units each (Fig. 5–31) and press the seams. Sew the rows together (Fig. 5–32) and press the seams. You did it! The block should measure 12½" x 12½" square.

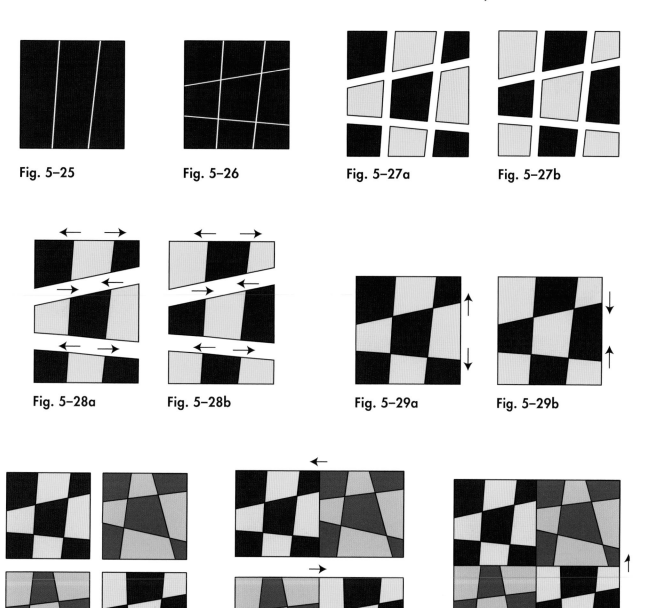

Fig. 5–25   Fig. 5–26   Fig. 5–27a   Fig. 5–27b

Fig. 5–28a   Fig. 5–28b   Fig. 5–29a   Fig. 5–29b

Fig. 5–30   Fig. 5–31   Fig. 5–32

Skill Builder Set 6
Improvisation

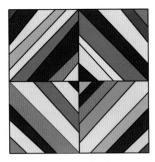

String Block

Asterisk Block

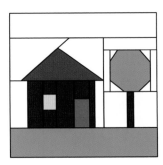

House and Tree Block

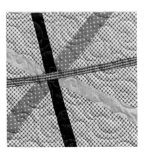

mprovisation is the practice of sewing fabric together without a set pattern. While improvisational piecing has happened on a small scale throughout the years, the showing of the Quilts of Gee's Bend in 2002 brought the technique back into the spotlight. The Gee's Bend quilters included four generations of African-American women from a small isolated town in Alabama who used a mix of traditional and improvisational techniques to make quilts.

Their quilts, made from old clothes and scraps, are utilitarian, graphic, and bold. The style is more like modern abstract art than traditional quilting. Their quilts and story inspires quilters and non-quilters alike. The concurrent rise of the modern quilt movement, characterized by bold colors, high contrast, negative space, and improvisational and minimalistic piecing, also gave improvisational quilting a new life.

Some people love the freedom of improvisational piecing. Others are uncomfortable with the lack of patterns and rules. Both responses are equally valid. We don't have to love everything as quilters, but give it a try. You just might find a new love.

Materials

(4) 6½" x 6½" squares of copy paper or lighter-weight foundation-piecing paper

Pins or a glue stick

Construction

Using a ruler and rotary cutter, cut (4) 6½"x 6½" squares from the paper. Cutting paper with a rotary cutter will not dull it. The paper is easier to remove when it is pierced more often with the sewing needle. Decrease the stitch length on the sewing machine so it sews 18–20 stitches per inch. This is a 1.5 setting on most machines.

String Block

The String Block is pieced on paper that keeps the strings (strips) of fabric from stretching as they are sewn together. The paper is torn from the back of the block prior to quilting. Using a small stitch length will make it easier to tear the paper off. Use whatever size of strings you like and sew them on at any angle you like. The only musts are that the strings lie flat on the paper, are sewn with a ¼" seam, and that the paper foundation is completely covered with strings.

Fabric

Choose a variety of colors.

Cutting

Strips of various widths and as long as 10".

Tip

Use 4 strings of the same color for the center diagonals to create an on-point square for visual pop.

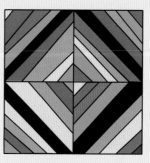

Fig. 6–1

Place a fabric string right side up along the diagonal on a paper square (Fig. 6–2, page 56). It doesn't have to be perfectly centered unless you want it to be. Attach the string to the paper with pins or a few dabs of washable glue stick. Place a

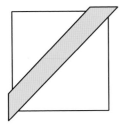

Fig. 6–2

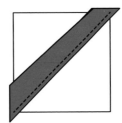

Fig. 6–3

Fig. 6–4

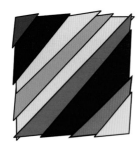

Fig. 6–5

Fig. 6–6

Fig. 6–7

second string on top of the first with right sides together (Fig. 6–3). Its edge can line up with the first string or it can be placed at an angle for a wonkier look. Sew a ¼" seam along the edge of the second string. Set the seam and then press open (Fig. 6–4).

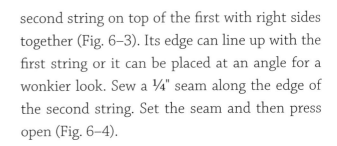

> ### Tip
>
> Make sure the strings are pressed flat against the paper before you add new strings. Sometimes they can shift and make bubbles of fabric. When the foundation paper is removed, the bubbles will flatten and cause the block to end up too large. Nice and flat is the goal.

Continue adding strings until the entire paper square is covered (Fig. 6–5). You can use the extra triangles from the Card Trick block for the last string to cover the corners if you wish. When the paper is completely covered, turn it over (Fig. 6–6). Using the paper as a guide, trim it to 6½" x 6½" square (Fig. 6–7). Repeat to make 4 string units. You can chain piece and press for greater speed.

Assembly

Without removing the paper, lay out the 4 string units in 2 rows of 2 units each (Fig. 6–8). Position them as illustrated or make your own layout. Sew them together into rows (Fig. 6–9) and then join the rows together (Fig. 6–10).

Carefully remove the paper. Start at one corner of the block, fold back the paper in the corner, crease, and carefully tear it off. Pull up the next strip of paper, crease, and tear off. Continue until all the paper has been removed. You can use a pair of tweezers to remove any small stubborn pieces of paper. You did it! Measure and trim the block to 12½" x 12½" square.

Fig. 6–8

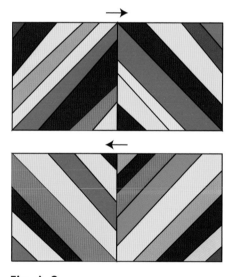

Fig. 6–9

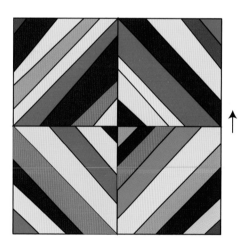

Fig. 6–10

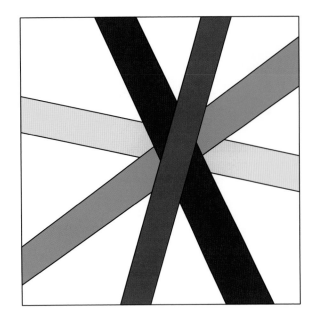

Asterisk Block

This block uses a fun technique. Simply cut the fabric apart and sew a strip of fabric between the two pieces. You can use this method in many different improvisational blocks.

Fabric

5 strips of contrasting colors, 1" – 2½" wide x 18"

Cutting

Fabric A   (1) 14" x 14" for the background

Fabrics B, C, D, and E
              (1) 1" x 16" strip from each fabric

> ### Tip
> Heavily starch the background fabric before beginning to make the block. This will help reduce stretching along the bias cuts.

Construction

Using a ruler and rotary cutter, cut across the Fabric A background square at any angle you wish (Fig. 6–11). Sew a string to a cut edge of the square (Fig. 6–12). Set the seam and press the seam allowance toward the string. Sew the opposite side of the square to the string (Fig. 6–13). Set the seam and press toward the string.

Make another angled cut (Fig. 6–14). Sew a string to a side of the cut (Fig. 6–15). Set the seam and press toward the string. Line up the other half of the square so the first string is straight across the block (Fig. 6–16). Flip the pieces one on top of the other and pin parallel to the edge of the fabric at the seam allowance (Fig. 6–17). Carefully open the 2 pieces to see if the first string visually joins its other half straight across the block. It may not be perfect; that is okay. If it is so far off that it bugs you, reposition the pieces. Sew the seam and press toward the second string.

Make a third cut (Fig. 6–18). For it to look like the example block, it should cut across the intersection of the first 2 strings. Of course, since this is improvisation, feel free to make the cut wherever you think this string would look best. Sew it to the cut edge (Fig. 6–19). Press the string and sew the other half of the block to it. Press the seam. Make the fourth cut and add the last string (Figs. 6–20 and 6–21). Trim the block to 12½" x 12½" square (Figs. 6–22 and 6–23). You did it!

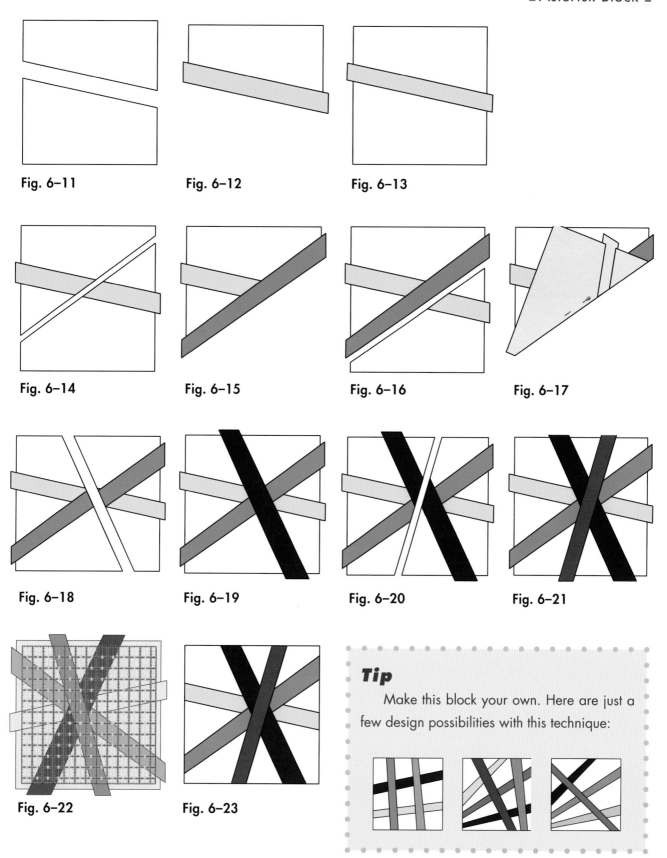

Fig. 6–11　　Fig. 6–12　　Fig. 6–13

Fig. 6–14　　Fig. 6–15　　Fig. 6–16　　Fig. 6–17

Fig. 6–18　　Fig. 6–19　　Fig. 6–20　　Fig. 6–21

Fig. 6–22　　Fig. 6–23

Tip

Make this block your own. Here are just a few design possibilities with this technique:

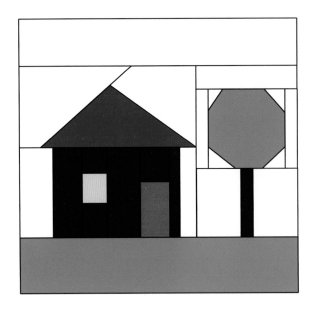

Fabric

Scraps of several fabrics

Construction
Making a House

Cut a piece of fabric 1"–2" larger than the desired size of the body of the house. Make 2 vertical cuts where you want the door (Fig. 6–24). Make a horizontal cut where you want the top of the door to be. Use the lower cut piece as a template and cut out a door piece slightly longer than the cut piece (Fig. 6–25). Sew the door piece to the house piece above it (Fig. 6–26). Press the seam allowance in this and subsequent seams toward the darker fabrics. Sew the house sides to the door piece (Fig. 6–27). Make the window using the same steps as the door (Figs. 6–28a–d). Add the background pieces to each side of the house (Figs. 6–29a and b).

Making a Roof

Cut a roof-shaped triangle with a base 1"–2" wider than the base of the house (Fig. 6–30). Lay the triangle on top of a large piece of background fabric right sides up (Fig. 6–31). Cut along one side of the triangle that extends to the edge of the background fabric (Fig. 6–32). Make another cut along the opposite edge of the triangle ending at the first cut (Fig. 6–33). Remove the resulting background fabric triangle.

Sew the roof triangle onto the background piece made from the second cut (Fig. 6–34). Sew the other background piece to the opposite side of the triangle (Fig. 6–35). Trim the bottom of the roof piece and the top of the house unit straight and sew them together (Figs. 6–36a and b).

House and Tree Block

There are no set measurements for the pieces of this block, just a series of pictures to help you envision how to make your own house and tree. Make them tall or short, wide or thin. Make 2 houses or all trees, the choice is yours!

> ### Tip
>
> Not sure where to start? Uncomfortable with improvisation? It may help to draw the design on graph paper first. Cut it out and add ¼" seam allowances around all of the pieces when cutting the fabrics. Here is a chance to make an original design.

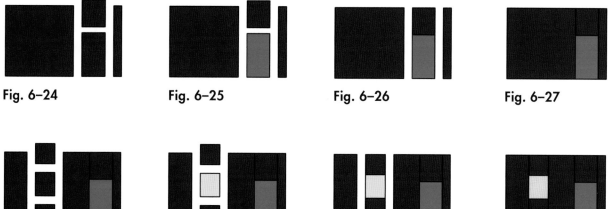

Fig. 6–24   Fig. 6–25   Fig. 6–26   Fig. 6–27

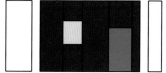 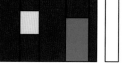 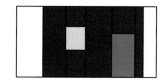

Fig. 6–28a   Fig. 6–28b   Fig. 6–28c   Fig. 6–28d

Fig. 6–29a   Fig. 6–29b

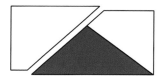 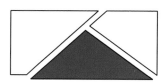

Fig. 6–30   Fig. 6–31   Fig. 6–32   Fig. 6–33

  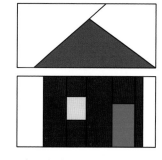 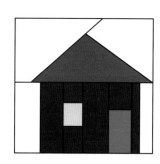

Fig. 6–34   Fig. 6–35   Fig. 6–36a   Fig. 6–36b

Making a Tree

Cut a piece of fabric ½" larger than the desired width and height of the treetop. Cut 4 squares that are between ⅓–½ the width of the treetop (Fig. 6–37). Place the squares on each corner of the treetop fabric and sew from one corner to the other in a straight line (Fig. 6–38). Trim off the corners (Fig. 6–39) and press the seam allowance outward (Fig. 6–40). Trim the unit so the sides are straight (Fig. 6–41). Add background pieces to both sides of the treetop (Fig. 6–42).

Cut a piece of fabric for the trunk ½" larger than the desired width and height (Fig. 6–43). Sew background pieces to either side of the trunk (Fig. 6–44). Make sure the trunk unit is at least as wide as the treetop unit. Trim the bottom of the treetop and the top of the trunk units so they are straight and sew them together (Fig. 6–45). Add background pieces to the top and bottom of the tree unit if necessary to make it as tall as the house unit (Fig. 6–46). Trim and straighten the edges of the tree unit (Fig. 6–47).

Sew the tree and house units together (Figs. 6–48a and b). Make sure the 2 units are at least 12½" wide but not so wide that parts of the house or tree will be cut off during the final trim. Add or remove background pieces as needed. Trim the top and bottom of the house and tree unit straight. Sew on strips of fabric for the grass and sky (Figs. 6–49a and b). Trim the block to 12½" x 12½" square (Figs. 6–50a and b). You did it! You made your own block!

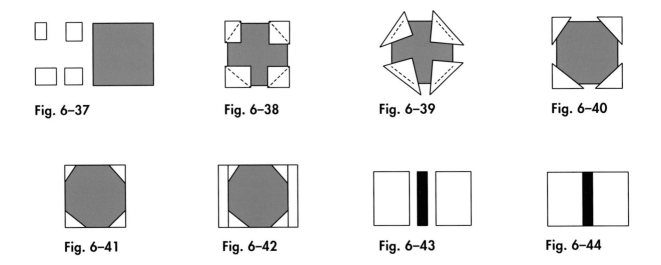

Fig. 6–37   Fig. 6–38   Fig. 6–39   Fig. 6–40

Fig. 6–41   Fig. 6–42   Fig. 6–43   Fig. 6–44

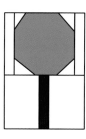

Fig. 6–45

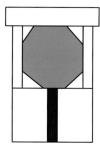

Fig. 6–46

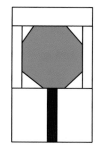

Fig. 6–47

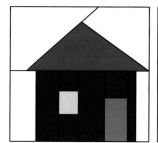

Fig. 6–48a

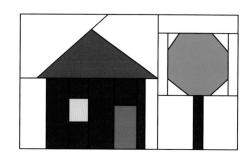

Fig. 6–48b

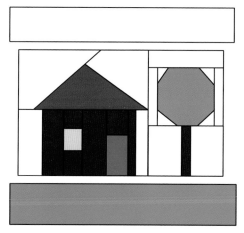

Fig. 6–49a

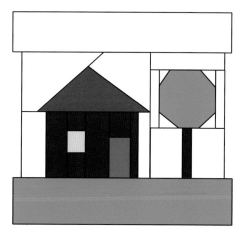

Fig. 6–49b

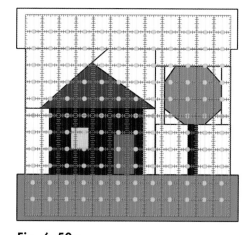

Fig. 6–50a

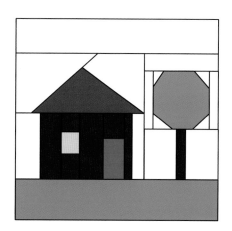

Fig. 6–50b

Skill Builder Set 7
Foundation Paper Piecing

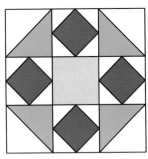

Hidden Star Block

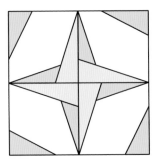

Eastern Star Block

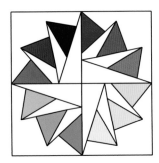

Circle of Geese Block

I n this chapter, we will work on developing foundation paper piecing skills. In foundation paper piecing, the outline of a quilt block pattern is printed on paper and fabric is sewn onto the paper using the lines as a sewing guide. When the block is complete, the paper foundation is removed. Amazingly accurate piecing is possible, even with the smallest of pieces.

The first step is to print or the paper foundation pattern onto a piece of paper and check that it is the correct size. You can use regular printer paper

or purchase specialty foundation paper, which is thinner and easier to see through and tear off after finishing the block. Unprinted newsprint is also easy to remove.

Always check that the pattern has printed to the correct size. Once you have determined that, you make as many copies as needed for your project. If using a printer, make sure you disable the "reduce or scale to size" option. As an extra check, measure the finished size of the block unit. If you know that the unit should measure 4" finished, make sure that it does (Fig. 7–1). All of the foundation paper piecing patterns in this book indicate the finished size of the units.

Next, prepare your fabric. Decide what fabric you want to use in each section and cut all pieces

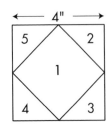

Fig. 7–1

as instructed. If there are many different pieces, you may want to label them by writing each section's number on a piece of paper and pinning them together (Fig. 7–2).

If you use a pattern that does not give cutting instructions, you can cut apart one paper foundation and use the pieces as templates (that is, patterns for cutting the fabrics). Cut the fabric at least ½" larger than the templates on each side. This is also a good option if you want to reduce the amount of fabric waste.

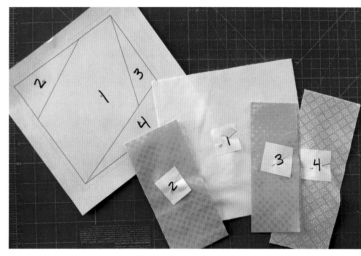

Fig. 7–2

Third, prepare your sewing machine by reducing the stitch length to 18–20 stitches per inch. This is a 1.5 setting on most sewing machines. The smaller stitch size will allow the paper to be pulled off easily when the block is finished. To determine what setting you should use, set your stitch length at 1.5 and sew on a piece of scrap fabric. Measure one inch of the sewing and count the number of stitches. If it is between 18 and 20, you are good to go. If not, adjust the stitch length until you have the correct setting for your machine.

Now you are ready to get started on the first block!

Tip

Find what works best for you. Most foundation paper piecing instructions will encourage stitching ¼"–½" beyond the sewing line and into the seam allowance. This usually requires tearing the paper foundation to add the next piece. Marlene does not routinely sew this extra stitching. Instead, she always locks the stitch at the start and the end of a seam, just as if you were hand quilting. This also keeps the paper from being ripped when adding the next piece.

Tip

An Add-a-Quarter™ ruler is especially helpful for paper piecing but a regular rotary ruler can also be used.

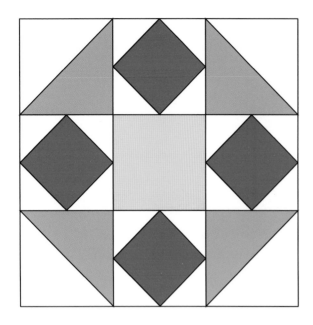

Hidden Star Block

The square-in-a-square unit can easily be made with traditional piecing but it is also perfect for practicing foundation paper piecing. Review the guidelines in the introduction to this chapter before getting started.

Foundations

Print 4 copies of the Hidden Star foundation on from the CD. Be sure they measure 4" x 4" plus ¼" on all sides for the seam allowances.

Fabric

Choose 4 contrasting colors (Fig. 7–3). If you use Fabric D on two adjacent corners of the paper-pieced unit, you will be able to see the Hidden Star more clearly (Fig. 7–4). Label the foundations with the fabric colors of your choice.

Cutting

Fabric A   (2) 5" x 5" squares
              (8) 3½" x 3½" squares cut
                  on the diagonal

Fabric B   (2) 5" x 5" squares

Fabric C   (4) 4½" x 4½" squares

Fabric D   (1) 4½" x 4½" square

To make the shape of the star more prominent, replace 4 of the 3½" x 3½" Fabric A squares with (4) 3½" x 3½" Fabric D squares. Cut on them on the diagonal and mark the paper foundations with new colors (Fig. 7–4)

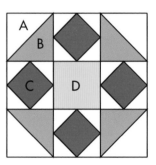

Fig. 7–3

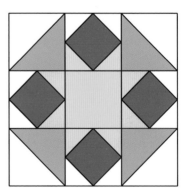

Fig. 7–4

Construction

All right, let's get piecing! Place the wrong side of a Fabric C square on the unmarked back of the paper foundation. Hold the foundation up to a light to ensure the fabric covers the entire area of the section labeled 1. It must also overlap the other sections by at least ¼" on all of its sides (Fig. 7–5). When in place, pin the fabric to the paper or use a dab of glue stick. Placing fabric on the wrong side of the foundation takes some getting used to, but in time it will become habitual.

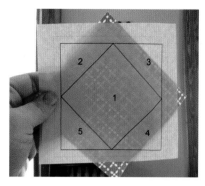

Fig. 7–5

Locate the line on the foundation that runs between section 1 and section 2. Using a postcard or piece of cardstock as a guide, fold the foundation back along the line between sections 1 and 2 (Figs. 7–6 and 7–7). Line up the ¼" line of a ruler with the folded edge of the paper (Fig. 7–8) and trim the exposed fabric to ¼". An Add-A-Quarter ruler (Fig. 7–9) has a lip at the ¼" mark to butt up against the folded paper and makes the trimming even easier.

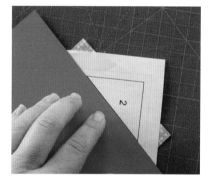

Fig. 7–6

Fold the foundation back down and flip it over. Place the second piece of fabric, a Fabric A triangle, right sides together on top of the first piece of fabric with the long edge of the triangle matched with the trimmed edge of the square (Fig. 7–10). Pin into place. As you get used to this technique you may not need a pin, but it is helpful to keep the fabric aligned.

Fig. 7–7

Flip the foundation over to the printed side. Set the stitch length

Fig. 7–8

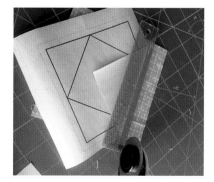

Fig. 7–9

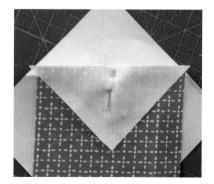

Fig. 7–10

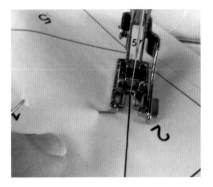

Fig. 7–11

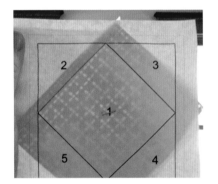

Fig. 7–12

Fig. 7–13

to 18–20 stitches per inch. Begin at the seam allowance line, lock the stitches, and sew on the line between sections 1 and 2 (Fig. 7–11). End at the opposite seam allowance line. Use the folded crease on the foundation as a sewing guide between the seam allowances and the seam line.

Repeat the steps above to trim and sew the first and second fabric pieces to the remaining foundations. Trimming, pinning, and sewing the same numbered section to multiple foundations, one after the other, speeds the process; you only have to figure out once which piece goes where.

Set the seam and press piece 2 open on all of the foundations. If the paper starts to curl up or brown, the iron is too hot and needs to be turned down. Hold the foundations up to the light and make sure the fabric covers all of section 2, including the seam allowances (Fig. 7–12).

To add the third fabric piece, place the cardstock on the line between section 3 and section 1 (Fig. 7–13). Fold the foundation over the card. Fabric will sometimes pull up with the foundation and that is fine (Fig. 7–14); simply pull the fabric gently off of the paper (Fig. 7–15). Using the folded edge of the paper as a guide, trim the exposed fabric to ¼". Repeat for all foundations.

Fold the foundation back down; match the long edge of the third fabric piece with the newly trimmed edge (Fig. 7–16). Pin if needed, flip, and sew.

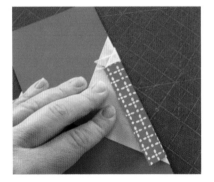

Fig. 7–14

Fig. 7–15

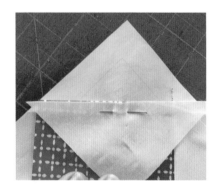

Fig. 7–16

Start and finish sewing at the seam allowance line. Repeat for the remaining foundations. Press piece 3 open.

Repeat these steps for pieces 4 and 5 to complete the foundations. The basic foundation piecing formula is to trim, sew, and press. It is that simple. As you go, hold the foundation up to a light to make sure the fabric covers all of the sections and seam allowances completely (Fig. 7–17).

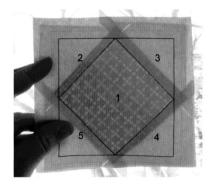

Fig. 7–17

Match the outer solid lines of the foundations with the ¼" line on the ruler and trim off the excess paper and fabric (Figs. 7–18 and 7–19). The cut will be much more accurate when measured ¼" from the outer solid line than if the ruler is lined up on the outer line.

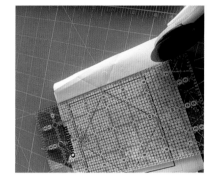

Fig. 7–18

To make the half-square triangle units (Fig. 7–20) for the corners of the Hidden Star block, draw a diagonal line (a) on the 5" x 5" squares of Fabric A. Place a Fabric A square right sides together with a 5" x 5" Fabric B square. Sew ¼" from both sides of the line (b). You can sew these seams with a normal stitch length but be sure to reduce it again when sewing on foundation paper. Cut on the line (c), press the halves open, and trim them to 4½" x 4½" square. If needed, refer to pages 25-26 for information on trimming. Make 4 half-square triangle units.

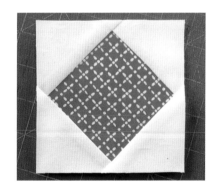

Fig. 7–19

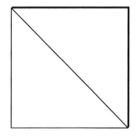

Fig. 7–20a

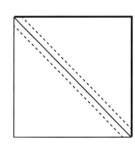

Fig. 7–20b

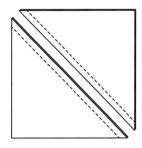

Fig. 7–20c

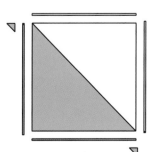

Fig. 7–20d

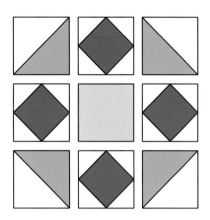

Fig. 7–21

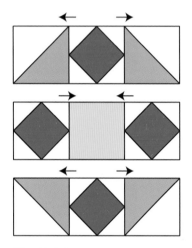

Fig. 7–22

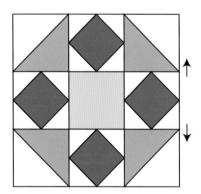

Fig. 7–23

Assembly

Lay out all of the block units in 3 rows of 3 units each (Fig. 7–21). Join them together into rows (Fig. 7–22). Use the solid outer lines on the paper-pieced units as a sewing guide. This will ensure that the points are not cut off. Press the seams toward the half-square triangles and the center block. Pin and sew the rows together (Fig. 7–23) and press. Leave the paper in place to ensure the block keeps its shape until it is joined to other blocks and then carefully remove the papers. You did it! Check to make sure that the block measures 12½" x 12½" square.

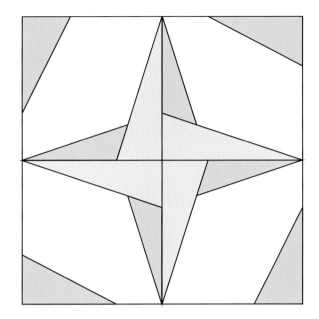

Eastern Star Block

The beautiful Eastern Star block has a fun secondary pattern that appears when a number of them are sewn together. It is made in four sections, which are then joined together. It is a step up in difficulty from the Hidden Star in that each piece and angle is different, but if you pay attention to which piece goes where and take your time, it should go together easily. Remember to trim, sew, and press and you will be just fine. Don't worry if the paper foundation seems backwards. Because the foundation is printed on the opposite side of the paper from the resulting block, the foundation is a mirror image of the finished block.

Foundations

Make 4 copies of the Eastern Star foundation on the CD (Fig. 7–24). Be sure they measure 6" x 6" plus ¼" on all sides for the seam allowances. Label the fabrics with the section numbers (Fig. 7-25).

Fabric

Choose 2 shades of a color for the star and a third one for the background (Fig. 7–25).

Cutting

Background fabric

Cut (4) 7½" x 7½" squares

Darker shade

Cut (4) 3" x 6½" rectangles for the corners

Cut (4) 2½" x 6½" rectangles for the short star spikes

Lighter shade

Cut (4) 3" x 8" rectangles for the long star spikes

Fig. 7–24

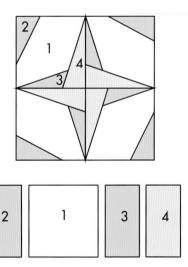

Fig. 7–25

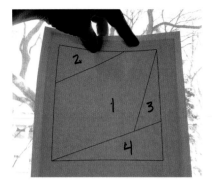

Fig. 7–26

Fig. 7–27

Fig. 7–28

Construction

See pages 64–65 for additional tips on foundation paper piecing.

Reduce the stitch length on the sewing machine. Place fabric piece 1 right-side up on the unprinted side of the paper foundation and attach it with a few dabs of glue or pins. Since this piece is so large, pin or glue along each side to keep the fabric from shifting. Hold the foundation up to a light to make sure the fabric covers all of section 1 including the outer seam allowances (Fig. 7–26). Using cardstock as a guide (Fig. 7–27), fold the foundation back on the line that runs between sections 1 and 2 (Fig. 7–28). Trim the exposed fabric to ¼" (Fig. 7–29).

Flip the foundation over and lay fabric piece 2 right-side down along the trimmed edge of fabric piece 1 (Fig. 7–30). Check to make sure it will cover the entire section 2 area and then pin it into place. Flip the foundation over and stitch on the line between sections 1 and 2 (Fig. 7–31). Set the seam and press fabric piece 2 open.

Fig. 7–29

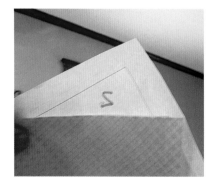

Fig. 7–30

Fig. 7–31

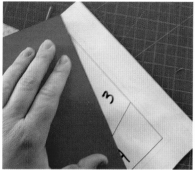

Fig. 7–32

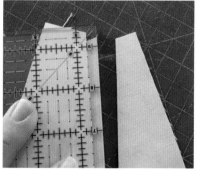

Fig. 7–33

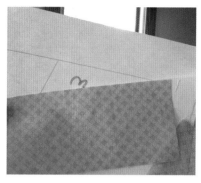

Fig. 7–34

Use the cardstock to fold the foundation back along the line between sections 1 and 3 (Fig. 7–32). Trim (Fig. 7–33) and then pin fabric piece 3 to the trimmed fabric (Fig. 7–34). Stitch on the line. Add fabric to section 4 in the same manner and repeat to finish all 4 templates.

Trim the excess paper and fabric ¼" from the solid line that outlines each paper foundation. Each unit should measure 6½" x 6½" square. They don't look like much alone, but when put together, you have a beautiful star.

Tip

Marlene prefers to start sewing at the point where lines 3 and 4 intersect, lock the stitch, and then proceed outward across the foundation and through the seam allowance beyond the finished edge. Stitching over an intersection inside of a foundation makes it more difficult to press out odd angles.

Tip

Use the needle test to make sure the foundation-paper units are lined up perfectly before sewing. Pin the units together, place them under the foot of the sewing machine, and lower the needle so it pierces the sewing line (Fig. 7–35). If the hole appears on the line on the other side, then the pieces are lined up perfectly. If not, (Fig. 7–36) adjust the pieces.

Fig. 7–35

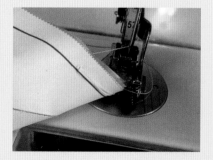

Fig. 7–36

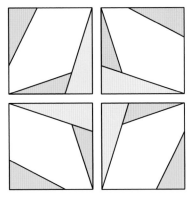

Fig. 7–37

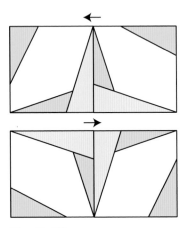

Fig. 7–38

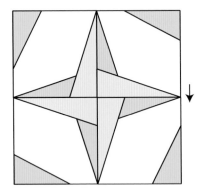

Fig. 7–39

Assembly

Lay out the units in 2 rows of 2 units each, paying attention to their orientation (Fig. 7–37). Pin the top 2 units together at each end, then in the middle. Pinning at the ends first will ensure they line up correctly. Sew together (Fig. 7–38). Repeat these steps for the bottom 2 units.

Pin the top and bottom rows together (Fig. 7–39). Start at the outside and work toward the center. This helps work in any extra ease. Use the needle test (see the tip on page 73) to make sure they are aligned properly and then sew the rows together. The block should measure 12½" x 12½". You did it!

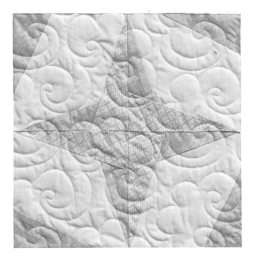

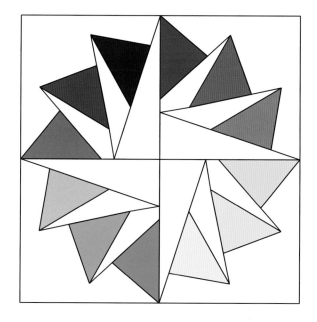

Circle of Geese Block

This block, designed by Beth Maddocks, motivated Leila to learn how to foundation paper piece. The movement is lovely, and with arrangements of different colors, the block can have many possible colorways.

Foundations

Make 4 copies of the Circle of Geese foundation on the CD. If you would prefer a counterclockwise rotation of geese, make a mirror image of the template.

Fabric

Choose 1–12 colors for the geese and 1 for the background.

Cutting

Goose Piece 1 Cut (12) 3" x 4½" rectangles for sections 1, 4, and 7

Background Piece 2 Cut (4) 3" x 4" rectangles

Background Piece 3 Cut (4) 2" x 5½" rectangles

Background Piece 5 Cut (4) 4" x 5" rectangles

Background Piece 6 Cut (4) 2" x 6½" rectangles

Background Piece 8 Cut (4) 2½" x 7½" rectangles

Background Piece 9 Cut (4) 3" x 8" rectangles

It is vital to label the different pieces of fabric with the section numbers for this block. There are so many pieces of the same color and similar size that it is easy to get confused which piece to use where (Fig. 7–41).

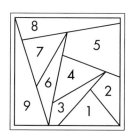

Fig. 7–40

Fig. 7–41

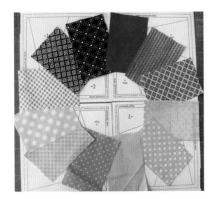

Fig. 7–42

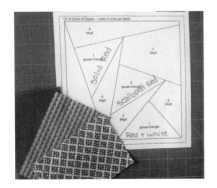

Fig. 7–43

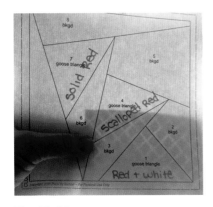

Fig. 7–44

Construction

Reduce the stitch length on the sewing machine. Arrange the paper foundations so the geese are flying in a circle. Lay the geese fabrics on top of the geese sections as desired (Fig. 7–42). With a pen or pencil (a wax-based marker will melt when ironed) write the name or color of each fabric on the appropriate goose section (Fig. 7–43). This will help ensure the fabrics end up where they belong.

Place fabric piece 1 right-side up on the unprinted back of the paper foundation and attach with a few dabs of glue or pins. Hold the foundation up to a light and check that the fabric covers all of section 1 plus at least a ¼" seam allowance all the way around it (Fig. 7–44).

Flip the foundation over and lay fabric piece 2 right-side down along the trimmed edge of fabric piece 1. Make sure it will cover all of section 2 and then pin it into place. Flip the foundation over and stitch on the line between sections 1 and 2. Set the seam and press fabric piece 2 open.

Continue adding pieces in numerical order. Check to make sure each piece will cover its section when opened. There are more pieces in this block but you aren't doing anything new. Just take it slow and steady and double-check the fabric numbering and color placement. You will be fine.

It is especially a good idea to sew the 4 foundations at the same time. Once you know how to place one piece of fabric, it is easy to repeat it for all them. Complete all 4 foundations and trim. Arrange the units as desired and finish the block as a four-patch (Figs. 7–45a, b, and c). The block should measure 12½" x 12½". You did it!

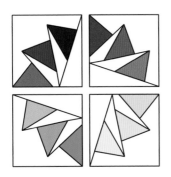

Fig. 7–45a

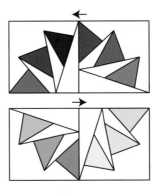

Fig. 7–45b

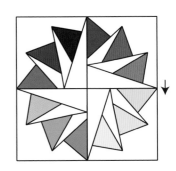

Fig. 7–45c

Skill Builder Set 8
Curves

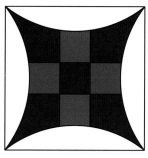

Curved Nine Patch Block

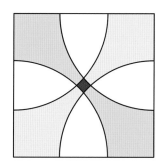

Flowering Snowball Block

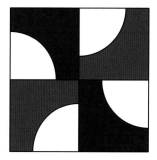

Drunkard's Path Block

As quilters, we tend to specialize in straight-line sewing; venturing into curves can be scary, intimidating, and seemly impossible to master. It is possible though, and even enjoyable, to sew blocks with curves. There are so many beautiful ones it would be a shame to not make any just because we were too scared to try.

Don't worry if the first curved blocks aren't perfect. No one expects to paint like Van Gogh the first time they pick up a paint brush and no one should expect their first curves to be perfect, either. We will use templates instead of rotary cutting. With a few basic steps to using a template, you will be making perfect curves in no time.

Preparing and Using a Template

There are two basic methods for making a template. The first is to trace a print of the desired template shape onto cardstock. All the templates are found on the CD that accompanies this book. Like the templates for foundation paper piecing, check to make sure the copy is the same size as the original. Using cardstock for templates is appropriate when just a few blocks are to be made. Over time and use, though, cardstock can lose its shape.

To make multiple blocks, using thin, clear template plastic is more appropriate. Sold in most fabric stores, it is thin enough to be cut with scissors but tough enough to stand up to multiple tracings. It is convenient to store for later projects and, because it is clear, you can position the template over a specific fabric motif to highlight or fussy cut (Fig. 8–1, page 78).

Fig. 8–1

Trace the desired shape onto template plastic and mark both the ¼" seam allowance (outer solid line) and the seam (inner dashed line) with a fine-point permanent marker. These lines will help center a highlighted motif to avoid sewing its edges into the seam. Cut out the template on the outer dashed line.

> **Tip**
>
> To trace straight lines, make a dot at both ends of the line; use a ruler to connect the dots. For curved tracing, making closely spaced dots along the line allows more control than tracing a line.

Heat-resistant Mylar™ can be used for templates; you can copy or print directly on it with a printer. If using an ink-jet printer, set the ink by placing paper directly on the printed side of the Mylar and pressing it with an iron at the wool setting for 5–10 seconds. Allow the template to cool before cutting it out.

Using a Template

Place a template on the fabric and trace around it. The templates can be traced with a removable-marking pen, but using a regular pen or pencil makes a finer line and moves easier over the fabric. Use a sharp pair of scissors to cut the template out just on the inside of the traced line. This will keep the fabric from becoming larger than the original template.

Align the straight edges of the template with the fabric grain (Fig. 8–2). Tracing can be simplified by precutting the straight edges with a rotary cutter and ruler. Tracing the entire template onto the fabric is necessary when all sides of the template are curved.

For example, with the Drunkard's Path block, match the corners of the templates with the corners of a precut square or rectangle of fabric. This minimizes the time spent tracing, cutting with scissors, and avoids inaccuracies (Fig. 8–3).

To avoid tracing and cutting with scissors, place the template on the fabric, place a rotary ruler on the straight edges of the template, and cut those first. Then use a small 18mm rotary cutter to carefully cut the curved sections.

Sewing

As you ease curved seams together, a scant ¼" seam is vitally important. When the seam is pressed, there will be some excess fabric along the seam line due to the curved edge. The scant ¼" provides a little extra space to make sure the end result is correct.

There are two ways to sew the pieces together—pinned or unpinned. To pin, find the seam line mid-point on both fabric pieces; pin them together at the mid-point and then pin them at the start and end of the seam. Continue adding pins until you feel there are enough.

To sew without pinning, match two pieces of fabric at the start of the seam with the convex curved piece on top and sew. Line up the next finger's width of the seam and sew several more stitches. Sew the seam in this manner until you reach the end. Be careful because curved seams are on the bias; stretching them will distort the shape. Instead, allow the fabrics to ease into themselves a finger's width at a time. Near the end of the seam, match the fabric edges before finishing the seam.

That's all you need to know for now about templates and curves. Let's get sewing!

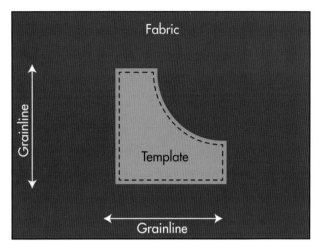

Fig. 8–2

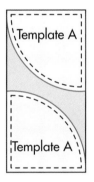
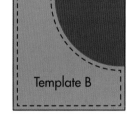

Fig. 8–3

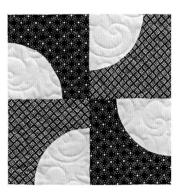

Tip

Steam and ironing can distort the fabric, however, if the quilt block is already distorted (curves can do that) these techniques can also help restore the block's shape. The more practice you get with sewing curves, the less likely you will need this trick but it can be helpful when first starting out.

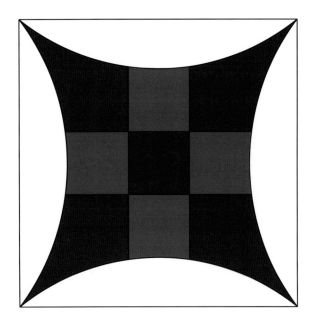

Curved Nine Patch Block

The gentle arcs of the Curved Nine Patch block are perfect to start a curved-piecing journey.

Templates

Prepare the Curved Nine Patch Templates 1–3 (on the CD) by copying them onto cardstock or tracing them onto plastic. Cut them out on the outer line.

Fabric

Choose 3 contrasting colors.

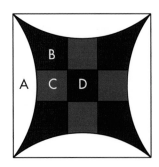

Fig. 8–4

Cutting

Fabric A   Cut (4) 12½" x 3" rectangles for Curved Nine Patch Template 1

Fabric B   Cut (4) 5½" x 5½" squares for Curved Nine Patch Template 2
Cut (1) 2⅞" x 2⅞" square for the center

Fabric C   Cut (4) 2⅞" x 2⅞" squares for Curved Nine Patch Template 3

Position the straight edges of the templates on the edges of the appropriate fabrics (Fig. 8–5); trace around the curved edges. Cut the pieces out on the inside of the traced line. Note that one side of Template 3 is curved.

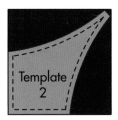

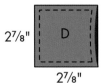

Fig. 8–5

Construction

Lay out the pieces of the center (Fig. 8–6). Sew them together into 3 rows of 3 pieces each (Fig. 8–7). Press the seams toward the darker fabric. Match the seams and sew the rows together (Fig. 8–8). Press the seam allowances in the direction of the arrows.

Find the midpoint of a curved side of the center unit by folding it in half. Use a fingernail to make a sharp crease. With the Template 1 piece on top, match the mid-point of the center unit with the mid-point of the Template 1 piece; pin them together (Fig. 8–9). Match and pin the outer ends of the seams together (Fig. 8–10). Then pin from the outside in (Fig. 8–11).

Carefully sew a scant ¼" seam along the curved edge. A scant seam is just a thread or two narrower than a ¼" seam. Sew slowly and steadily, placing a finger in front of the foot to feel for and smooth any tucks or puckers. Press the seam allowance toward the Template 1 piece.

Repeat on the remaining 3 sides. Press the seams. If necessary, trim to 12½" x 12½" square. You did it! Was it as hard as you thought?

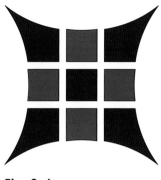

Fig. 8–6

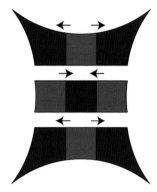

Fig. 8–7

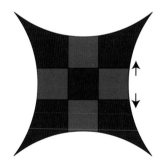

Fig. 8–8

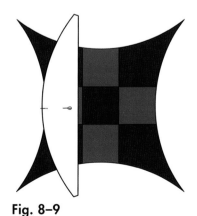

Fig. 8–9

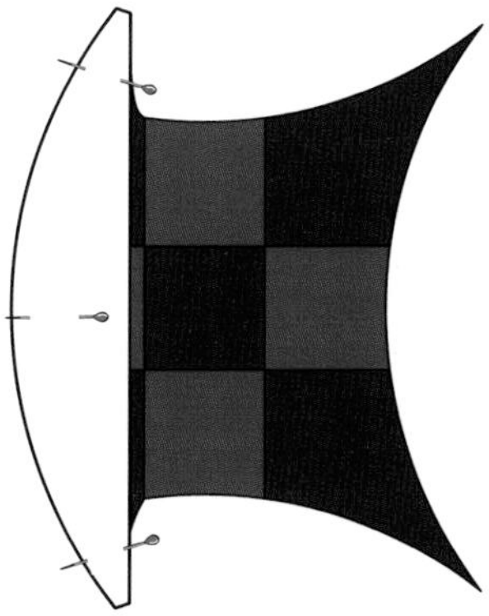

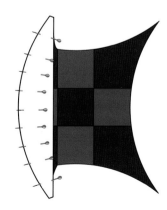

Fig. 8–10

Fig. 8–11

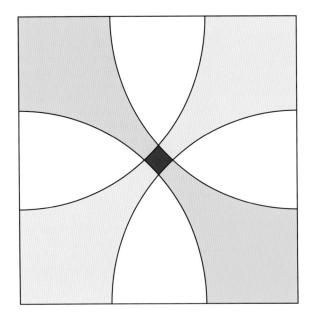

Flowering Snowball Block

The Flowering Snowball is an elegant block with a beautiful secondary design that emerges from the petals when used in large numbers. We are increasing the difficulty by sewing tighter curves and more of them, but you can handle it.

Templates

Prepare the Flowering Snowball Templates 1 and 2 (on the CD) by printing them onto cardstock or tracing them onto plastic. Cut them out on the outer line.

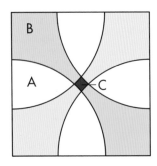

Fig. 8–12

Fabric

Choose 3 contrasting fabrics (Fig. 8–12). The coloration we chose includes white petals (A) and a multi-colored background. You may wish to have colored petals with a neutral background fabric for the B sections.

Cutting

Fabric A   Cut (4) 4½" x 5¾" rectangles for Flowering Snowball Template 1

Fabric B   Cut (4) 6¾" x 6¾" squares for Flowering Snowball Template 2

Fabric C   Cut (1) 2¼" x 2¼" square for Flowering Snowball Template 3

Position the templates at the edges of the appropriate fabrics (Fig. 8–13). Trace around the curved edges and cut the pieces out on the inside of the outer line.

 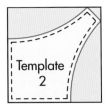

Fig. 8–13

Construction

Sew (2) Template 2 corner pieces to opposite sides of the Template 3 center square using a scant ¼" seam. Make 1 corner/center unit (Fig. 8–14). Press the seam allowance toward the center.

Place a Template 1 petal piece on top of an unsewn Template 2 corner piece with right sides together and line up the bottoms. Carefully pin them together at the bottom corner (Fig. 8–15). Pin the tip of the Template 1 piece to the top of the Template 2 piece. Working from the outside in, ease the edges together and pin (Fig. 8–16). Sew slowly, placing a finger in front of the foot to feel for and smooth any fabric tucks.

Sew another Template 1 petal piece to the other side of the Template 2 corner piece (Figs. 8–17a and b). Press toward the petals. Make 2 petal/corner units (Fig. 8–18).

Attach the petals/corner units to the corners/center unit. Match the seams and pin at the center (Fig. 8–19). Pin the outside corners together (Fig. 8–20). Pin the rest of the curve starting at the outside edges and working towards the center (Fig. 8–21).

Assembly

Sew the units together with a scant ¼" seam. Sew the other petals/corner unit to the other side of the corners/center unit. Press the seams toward the petals. You did it! Measure and trim the block to 12½" x 12½" square, if necessary.

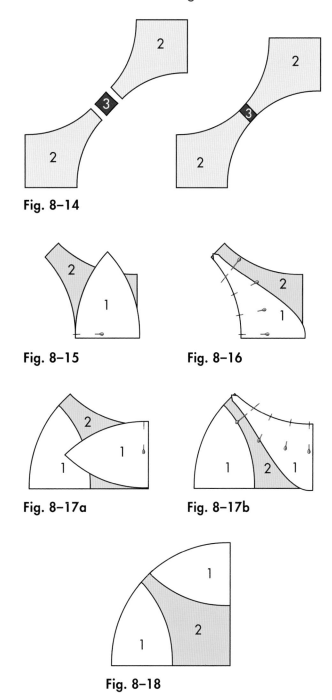

Fig. 8–14

Fig. 8–15

Fig. 8–16

Fig. 8–17a

Fig. 8–17b

Fig. 8–18

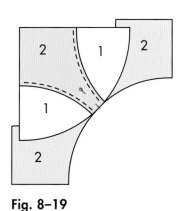

Fig. 8–19

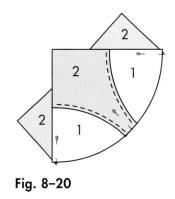

Fig. 8–20

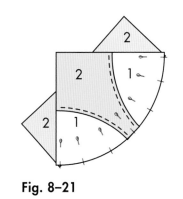

Fig. 8–21

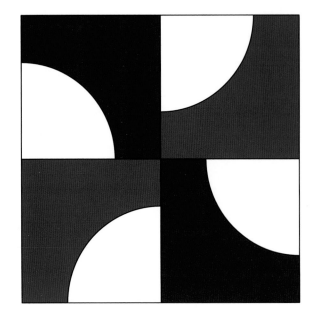

Drunkard's Path Block

The Drunkard's Path block has gone by many names over the years. One reason for its popularity is that there are many different secondary designs that can be made with its basic shape. The curves on this block are tighter than any we have done thus far, but are quite doable with careful pinning and sewing.

Templates

Prepare the Drunkard's Path Templates 1 and 2 (on the CD) by printing them onto cardstock or tracing them onto plastic. Cut them out on the outer line.

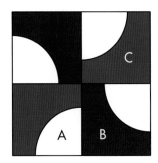

Fig. 8–22

Fabric

Choose 3 contrasting fabrics (Fig. 8–22).

Cutting

Fabric A   Cut (2) 4½" x 8½" rectangles for Drunkard's Path Template 1

Fabric B   Cut (2) 6½" x 6½" squares for Drunkard's Path Template 2

Fabric C   Cut (2) 6½" x 6½" squares for Drunkard's Path Template 2

Position Template 1 at opposite corners of the Fabric A rectangles and trace them (Fig. 8–23). Match the corners of Template 2 with the corners of the Fabric B and C squares and trace the curve (Fig. 8–24). Cut just inside the line.

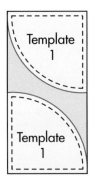

Fig. 8–23

Fig. 8–24

Construction

Fold a Template 1 piece and a Template 2 piece in half to find the center of each curve. Finger press a crease at the center of each. Match the creases and pin them together. Match the straight edges at the corners and pin. Add additional pins from the corners to the center (Figs. 8–25a and b).

Sew the curve with a scant ¼" seam. It is especially important to make sure the extra fabric is eased in front of the presser foot. Sew slowly and carefully, placing a finger in front of the foot to feel for and smooth any fabric tucks.

Press the seam allowance toward the Template 1 pieces. Repeat the steps above to make (4) Drunkard's Path units. Each unit should measure 6½" x 6½" square. Trim to size if needed.

Assembly

There are many possible layout variations with this block. Play around with the units to find the layout you prefer. Lay out the block units as shown (Fig. 8–26) or as desired. Sew them together into rows (Fig. 8–27). Press the seam allowance in the direction of the arrows. Match the center seam allowance and sew the rows together (Fig. 8–28). Press as shown.

Trim the block to 12½" x 12½" square, if necessary. You did it! You sewed curved blocks! The next chapter will provide more chances to hone curved-piecing skills. Are you ready?

Fig. 8–25a

Fig. 8–25b

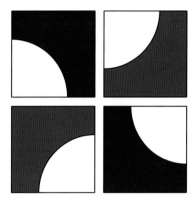

Fig. 8–26

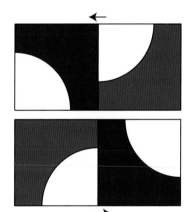

Fig. 8–27

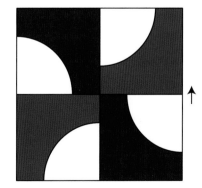

Fig. 8–28

Skill Builder Set 9
One-Patch Blocks

Tumbler Block

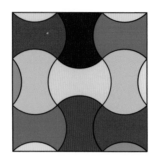

Apple Core Block

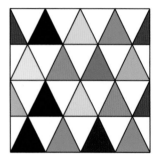

Triangle Block

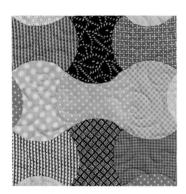

Some quilts are made completely with one-shape units. This simplicity lets the fabric be the star. These quilts are some of our favorites. We will start with the Tumbler block and then continue working with curves by making the Apple Core block. This is one of the more challenging blocks in this book, but you can do it! We will finish the chapter with the Triangle block.

All of these blocks use templates. If you want to make a complete quilt with any of these shapes, piece them into rows the length you need for the width of the quilt and then sew together as many rows as needed to obtain the length you want. If you use a different fabric for every patch, you've made a charm quilt!

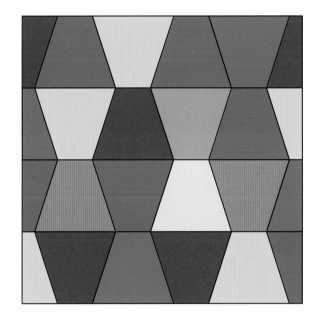

Tumbler Block

This one-patch block is simple to make and has a lot of personality.

Template

Prepare the Tumbler Template (on the CD) by copying it onto cardstock or tracing it onto plastic. Cut it out on the outer line. Detailed information for making templates is on pages 77–79.

Fabric

4 or more prints with good contrast

Cutting

Cut 3½" wide strips from various prints. A 3½" x 12" strip will make 3 tumbler pieces. Make 24 tumbler pieces using either the tracing or the rotary-cutting method described below.

Tracing

Position the tumbler template on the 3½" strips. Trace the template shape 24 times and cut them out just inside the outer line.

Rotary Cutting

Tape 2 templates to the back of a ruler with opposite edges of the templates at the edges of the ruler (Fig. 9–1). Match the top and bottom of the template on the right with the fabric strip. Cut along the edge of the ruler with a rotary cutter (Fig. 9–2). Match the cut edge with the inner edge of the template on the left. Match the top and bottom of the fabric to the template and cut (Fig. 9–3). Continue rotating the ruler and cutting until you have enough tumblers from that fabric.

Fig. 9–1

Fig. 9–2

Fig. 9–3

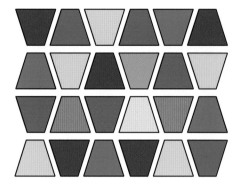

Fig. 9–4

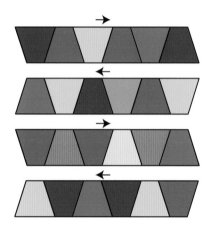

Fig. 9–5

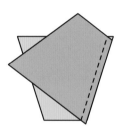

Fig. 9–6

> ### Tip
>
> If cutting with your left hand is difficult, rotate the mat between cuts in order to cut with your right hand. A rotating mat makes this a breeze.

Assembly

Lay out the tumblers in 4 rows of 6 units each (Fig. 9–4). To sew the rows together (Fig. 9-5), the points of the tumbler pieces need to overlap ¼" from the edge (Fig. 9–6). They are lined up correctly if the machine needle is both at the intersection of the fabrics and ¼" from the raw edge when you start sewing. Press the rows in opposite directions. Trim the dog ears. Straighten any waviness with a ruler and rotary cutter. Be careful not to trim the strip any narrower than 3½".

Pin the rows together. The seams will nest together making them easy to match. Sew the rows together (Fig. 9–7). Press the seams. Use a 12½" x 12½" square ruler to trim the edges (Fig. 9–8). You did it!

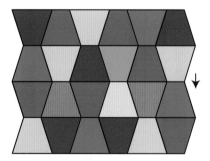

Fig. 9–7

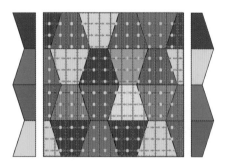

Fig. 9–8

YOU CAN QUILT! Building Skills for Beginners ● Leila Gardunia & Marlene Oddie

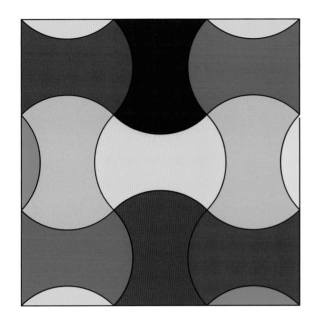

Apple Core Block

This block is challenging, especially if the apple cores are small. We will use a medium size core. Take it slowly, one seam at a time. You will do fine.

Templates

Prepare the Apple Core Templates 1 and 2 (on the CD) by printing them onto cardstock or tracing them onto plastic. Cut them out on the outer line.

Fabric

5–9 contrasting colors

Supplies

Removable marking pen

Cutting

(9) 7" x 5" rectangles of various fabrics for Apple Core Template 1

(6) 5" x 1½" rectangles of various fabrics for Apple Core Template 2

Because the apple core is curved on all sides, there are 2 ways to cut it. Trace the template onto fabric and cut it with scissors or stack several pieces of fabric together and use an 18mm rotary cutter to trim around the template. Be careful not to trim the template at the same time (Fig. 9–9).

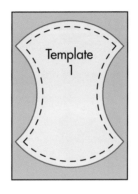

Fig. 9–9

Construction

Fold the apple cores and partial cores in half lengthwise. On the wrong side of the fabric, mark the center at both ends with a removable marker. Then fold them widthwise and mark the center on both sides (Fig. 9–10).

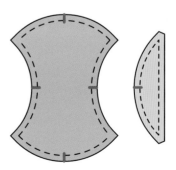

Fig. 9–10

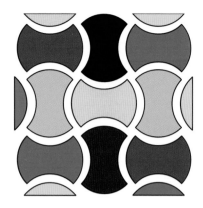

Fig. 9–11

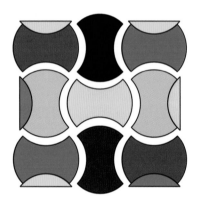

Fig. 9–12

Arrange the apple cores (Fig. 9–11). Pin the partial apple cores to the adjacent whole cores (Fig. 9–12). Match and pin the centers first (Fig. 9–13) and then pin the corners (Fig. 9–14).

Sew very slowly, stopping regularly with the needle down to adjust the fabric. Press the seams toward the partial pieces. Match the centers of the whole apple cores and pin (Fig. 9–15) and then pin the corners (Fig. 9–16). Sew the apple cores together into rows (Fig. 9–17). Press the seams toward the top (convex side) of the apple core.

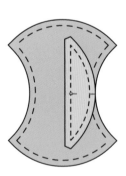

Fig. 9–13

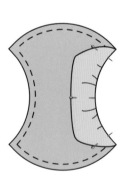

Fig. 9–14

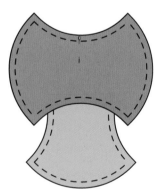

Fig. 9–15

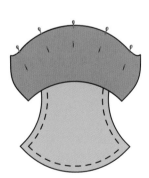

Fig. 9–16

Assembly

Match the seams of the rows together and pin. The seams should butt together, if not, press them again so that they will. Match and pin the centers. Place additional pins as needed. Slowly sew the rows together and stop as necessary to adjust the fabric.

Fan the seam intersections like a four-patch unit and press in alternating directions toward the apple core tops (Fig. 2-19, page 28) If the block does not lie flat, spritz lightly with water and press. Trim and square the block to 12½" x 12½" (Figs. 9–18a and b). You did it!

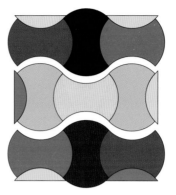

Fig. 9–17

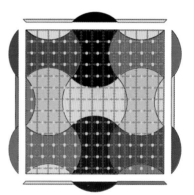

Fig. 9–18a

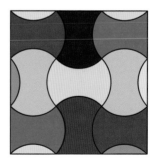

Fig. 9–18b

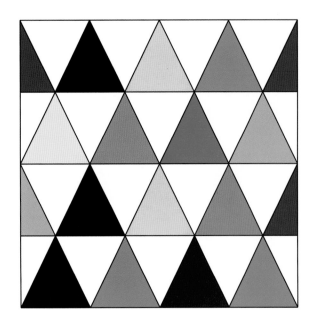

Triangle Block

Triangle quilts have a unique beauty in their simplicity. Triangles come in all shapes and sizes; as long as the two angles of the base are equal, the triangles will fit together into rows perfectly.

Template

Prepare the Triangle Template (on the CD) by printing it onto cardstock or tracing it onto plastic. Cut it out on the outer line.

Fabric

Choose a variety of colors.

Cutting

Cut 36 triangles from contrasting fabrics. We used 18 white and 18 assorted colors. Use either the tracing or the rotary cutting method. Cut 3½" strips from various prints.

Tracing

Cut 3½" strips from various prints and trace the template onto them. Cut on the lines. A 3½" x 9" strip will make 3 triangle pieces.

Rotary Cutting

Using the same method described for the Tumbler block on page 87, tape 2 triangle templates to the back of a ruler with opposite sides at the edges of the ruler and rotary cut 36 triangles.

Assembly

Arrange the triangles into 4 rows of 9 triangles each (Fig. 9–19). Sew them into rows (Fig. 9–20). The corners of the triangles will overlap the blunt end ¼" from the edge (Fig. 9–21). Press the rows in opposite directions. If using half white and half prints, press away from the white triangles.

Pin the rows together, matching the seams. Sew the rows together (Fig. 9–22). Remember to sew over the X made from piecing the triangles into rows (Fig. 9–23). This will ensure the points of the triangles are not sewn into the seams. Press the seams; trim and square the block to 12½" x 12½" (Fig. 9–24a and b). You did it!

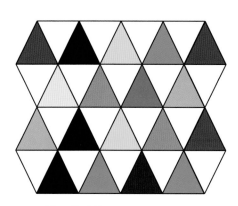

Fig. 9–19

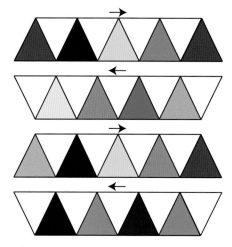

Fig. 9–20

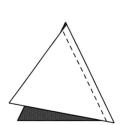

Fig. 9–21

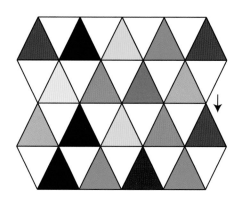

Fig. 9–22

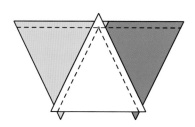

Fig. 9–23

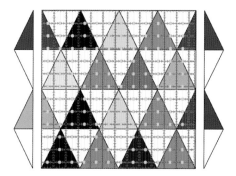

Fig. 9–24a

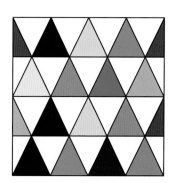

Fig. 9–24b

Skill Builder Set 10
Appliqué

Orange Peel Block

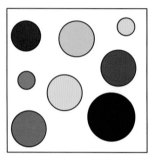

Circles Block

Tulip Cross Block

Appliqué is a form of piecing in which fabric shapes are cut and then stitched on top of a background fabric. Amazingly detailed designs are possible using appliqué. This chapter will introduce a few basic methods of appliqué. It does not pretend to be inclusive nor as detailed as appliqué books devoted to the subject, but it will get you on your way.

Leila's Story

When I first started quilting, I swore I would never do appliqué. Too tricky, time intensive, and tedious. When my sister-in-law was expecting her second child, my husband got it into his head that we should make the new baby a quilt with appliquéd clouds and a kite in the center. I told him I would do a pieced border but if he wanted an appliquéd center, he would have to make it himself. And he did!

He drafted the pieces and got to work. He stitched while we watched TV in the evenings and even worked on it in airports while traveling for work. Boy, did he get some funny looks but he finished it in time for the baby's birth. It wasn't perfect, but He Did It! I decided that if my husband, who had never picked up a needle except to sew on the occasional button, could appliqué then I could, too. I discovered that appliqué was a relaxing way to end the day, not a tedious chore. Who would have thought?

Not everyone will like appliqué and that is okay, but to not try because you are afraid you can't? Well, that is not acceptable and defeats the whole point of this book. Try new things! Overcome fears! If Leila's husband can do it, so can you!

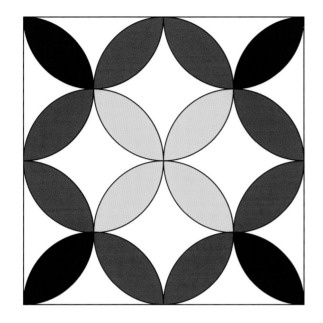

Fabric

Choose a variety of colors for the orange peels that will contrast well on the background color. If you wish to make the block pictured here, make 8 red peels, 4 yellow peels, and 4 blue peels. There are so many color choices possible with this block; you could make a monochromatic block, one with a rainbow of colors, or a scrappy one. The choice is yours (Figs. 10–1a, b, and c).

Cutting

Background fabric   Cut 13" x 13" square

Orange peels   Cut (16) 3" x 3" squares (Fig. 10–2). If you wish to make the block pictured left, cut 8 red, 4 yellow, and 4 blue peels

Supplies

Pen (not a disappearing one)

Lightweight double sided interfacing

Thread to match the appliqué fabrics or a clear monofilament thread

Orange Peel Block

The first method we will do is raw-edge appliqué. It is fairly simple and great for children's quilts because it is quick, durable, and strong.

Template

Prepare the Orange Peel Template (on the CD) by copying it onto cardstock or tracing it onto plastic. Cut it out on the outer line. This template does not have a seam allowance since we are doing raw-edge appliqué.

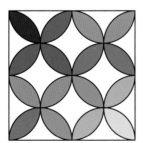

Fig. 10–1a

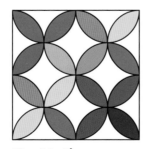

Fig. 10–1b

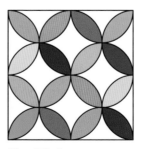

Fig. 10–1c

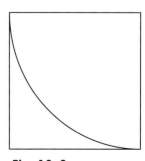

Fig. 10–2

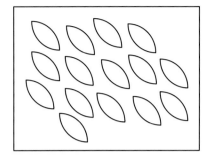

Fig. 10–3

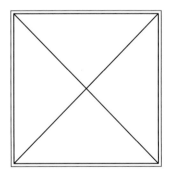

Fig. 10–4

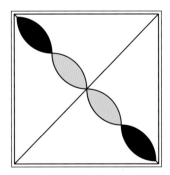

Fig. 10–5

Tip

If using a fusible web with paper on both sides, determine which of the two papers comes off more easily. Do Not Mark on that paper as it will be removed early in the appliqué process. Make all pattern marks on the other paper, the one bonded more firmly to the fusible web.

Construction

With a pen (not a pencil), trace the orange peel template 16 times onto the fusible web paper. Leave at least ¼" between each peel.

Cut the peels from the fusible web. Do not cut on the lines, instead, cut roughly around the peels leaving at least ⅛" outside the traced lines. Place them on the wrong side of the 3" x 3" fabric squares with the fusible web paper-side up. Iron following the instructions found on the fusible web. Cut out the peels just inside the line drawn on the paper (Fig. 10–3).

With a pencil or removable marking pen, draw a 12½" x 12½" square in the center of the background fabric square. Draw a line from corner to corner in both directions (Fig. 10–4). The lines will serve as guides for positioning the peels.

Smooth the background fabric on an ironing surface. Lay the peels next to the background and decide on a color arrangement that suits you. Remove the remaining paper from one of the peels in the center and place one point at the center of the background fabric and the other point along one of the diagonal lines. Touch the tip of the iron on the center of the peel. This will tack it in place. With the peel only partially attached, it is possible to pull it off and reposition it if needed.

Fig. 10–6a

Tip

If you are using Lite Steam-A-Seam2® fusible web, just finger press the peels into place for now.

Attach all of the peels along one diagonal (Fig. 10–5). The points of the peels in the outer corners should be ¼" from the sides of the square drawn on the background fabric (Fig. 10–6a and b). Attach the peels along the second diagonal. Add the side peels (Fig. 10–7a and b). One point should touch the points of the peels on the diagonals; the top points should touch each other ¼" from the edge of the square. Repeat for all 4 sides.

¼" from each side of the corner

Fig. 10–6b

With all of the peels positioned correctly and tacked down, lay a pressing sheet, parchment, or the paper removed from the interfacing over the top of the appliqué pieces. This sheet will protect the iron from interfacing that might seep out from under the appliqué pieces. Press according to the directions on the fusible web. Be sure all of the edges and points of the appliqués are completely fused to the background fabric. Use a matching thread color or a monofilament (clear) thread to stitch the edges of each peel.

Fig. 10–7a

There are many different ways to finish the edges of appliqué. Three common machine stitches used in raw-edge or turned-edge appliqué are zigzag, satin, and blanket stitches (Fig. 10–8a, b, and c). The ideal is for one edge of the stitch to barely go off the edge of the appliqué and into the background. The opposite side of the stitch goes into the appliqué.

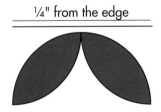

¼" from the edge

Fig. 10–7b

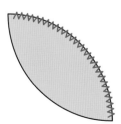

Fig. 10–8a

Fig. 10–8b

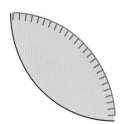

Fig. 10–8c

■ Appliqué ■
■ Orange Peel Block ■

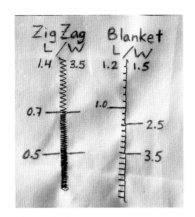

Fig. 10–9

Before starting to sew the peels to the background, take a scrap of fabric and experiment with the settings on the sewing machine; the higher the stitch width, the wider the stitch. Satin stitch is the same as a zigzag stitch but with a stitch length of almost 0. You may wish to label the scrap with the stitch lengths and widths used to make each stitch to keep as a future reference (Fig. 10–9). Leila zigzagged around her peels with a 0.5 length and a 3.5 width.

Fig. 10–12

Tip

To keep the points and corners of appliqués neat and sharp, stop with the needle down at the point. Lift the presser foot and rotate the fabric (Fig. 10–10) so the next stitch will come down in the middle of the appliqué (Fig. 10–11).

If the point is especially narrow and the stitching is wide, the stitching can go off the appliqué and into the background fabric when the fabric is rotated at the point with the needle down. To avoid this, use a narrower stitch all the way around the appliqué. This same technique will smooth the transition from stitching over the top of one peel to stitching on the bottom of the next peel.

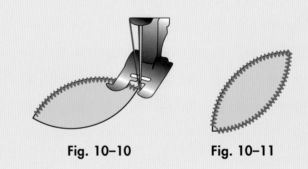

Fig. 10–10   **Fig. 10–11**

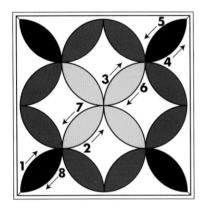

Fig. 10–13

Follow the stitching diagram (Fig. 10–12) for minimum starts and stops. Start at one corner of the block (1). Take a few stitches and backstitch. Start in the left upper corner of the block and stitch the top edge of the peel. As you approach the opposite point of the peel, guide the edge of the appliqué to the center of the zigzag stitching to ease the transition to the next peel. When you reach the opposite point, continue the stitching on the underside of the next peel in line (2).

Sew the alternating upper (3) and lower (4) sides of the peel diagonally across the block and stop with the needle down. Turn around and stitch the remaining sides of the peels until you reach the starting point (5–8). Backstitch just a few stitches. Repeat and sew the peels on the other diagonal (Fig. 10–13).

Stitch the peels around the edges of the block (Fig. 10–14). Start sewing at the top and follow the arrows all the way around. At the fabric edges (for example, between 2 and 3), stop with the needle down and rotate the block to stitch the next peel. When you reach the top again (Fig. 10–15), stop with the needle down, rotate the block, and stitch the underside of the peel (9). Follow the arrows around the block (9–16). Backstitch a few stitches when finished.

Trim and square the block to 12½" x 12½" making sure to leave the ¼" seam allowance beyond the orange peels. And you did it! We really like this block. Wouldn't it be fun to make a bunch and join them together into a large quilt?

Fig. 10–14

Fig. 10–15

Tip

When appliquéing larger shapes, removing the middle of the interfacing before ironing it to the fabric will reduce the stiffening of the appliqués. Trace the template onto the interfacing (Fig. 10–16). Roughly cut around the outer edges and the center of the shape (Fig. 10–17). Iron the interfacing to the back of the fabric (Fig. 10–18). Cut just inside the outer line on the interfacing, remove the paper, and iron the appliqué to the background (Fig. 10–19).

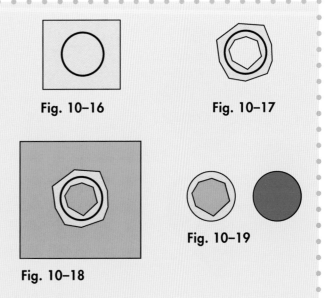

Fig. 10–16

Fig. 10–17

Fig. 10–18

Fig. 10–19

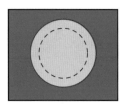

Fig. 10–20

Fig. 10–21

Fig. 10–22

Appliqué Methods

Raw-Edge Appliqué

The fabric is attached to the background with a fusible interfacing; the edges are not turned under. Templates used for raw-edge appliqué will not include seam allowances. This is the method used to appliqué the Orange Peel block. Some quilters don't finish the edges at all on art quilts or when the quilt will be used as a wallhanging.

Finished-Edge Appliqué

With this method, seam allowances are added to the drawn template shapes and the edges are turned under before or while the appliqué is attached. There are many ways to do this.

Needle-Turn Appliqué—
Line Drawn on the Appliqué

This is the traditional method for appliqué and is the best way to appliqué small, intricate pieces. Trace the template on the right side of the appliqué fabric (Fig. 10–20) and cut about ¼" outside the traced line (Fig. 10–21). Clip the outer curved edges, stopping 1–2 threads before the traced line (Fig. 10–22).

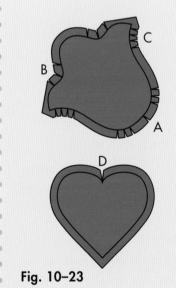

Fig. 10–23

Tip

To clip the seams (Fig. 10–23) when the appliqué has convex (outward) curves like a circle (a), cut a small triangle of fabric almost to the seam or traced line. This allows the fabric to fold back on itself without getting bulky or pleated. With concave (inward) curves shaped, which look like a bite out of a cookie (b), make slits so the fabric can spread as it is turned back on itself.

For exterior points (c), trim off the end almost to the point and angle the seams leading up to the point. With interior points (d), make a slit almost to the seam and turn under. When you get to the point, make a few extra stitches to secure the fabric.

Fig. 10–24

Fig. 10–25

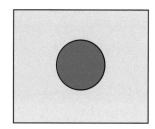

Fig. 10–26

Pin the clipped appliqué in place (Fig. 10–24). Using a needle, tuck the seam allowance under the appliqué and make a stitch. Learning how to turn the seam under with a needle takes practice. As a beginner, it may be easier to use both a finger and a needle. Continue hand stitching (Fig. 10–25), turning the seam allowance under along the traced line until the appliqué is completely stitched to the background fabric (Fig. 10–26).

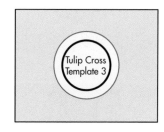

Fig. 10–27

Needle-Turn Appliqué—
Line Drawn on the Background

Trace the shape to be appliquéd directly on the background fabric (Fig. 10–27). Trace the shape on the back of the appliqué fabric and roughly cut it out ¼" larger than the traced shape (Fig. 10–28). Center the appliqué on top of the traced shape on the background fabric. Hold or pin the appliqué on the fabric. Turn under an edge of the appliqué, match it to the traced line on the background fabric, and catch the turned-under edge with a needle (Fig. 10–29). Stitch back down through the background fabric. Work around the traced background image, stitching and turning the appliqué under as you go (Fig. 10–30). Trim the edges of the appliqué if too much needs to be turned under.

Fig. 10–28

Fig. 10–29

Interfaced Appliqué

This method both turns under the edge and attaches the appliqué to the background fabric prior to stitching around the

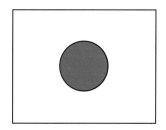

Fig. 10–30

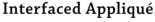

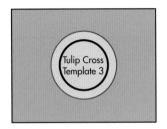

Fig. 10–31

Fig. 10–32

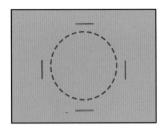

Fig. 10–33

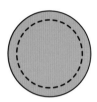

Fig. 10–34

Fig. 10–35

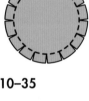

Fig. 10–36

Fig. 10–37

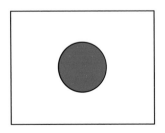

Fig. 10–38

edges. Trace the shape to be appliquéd onto the wrong side of the fabric (Fig. 10–31). Pin one-sided fusible interfacing right sides together with the appliqué fabric; the glue dots on the interfacing will face the right side of the fabric (Fig. 10–32). Using a regular stitch, sew on the line (or just inside the line) all the way around the appliqué (Fig. 10–33). If the appliqué is small with many curves and points, decrease the stitch length to provide more maneuverability and accuracy. Trim fabric to just under a ¼" (Fig. 10–34) and clip the seam allowance (Fig. 10–35).

Make a slit in the interfacing (Fig. 10–36); turn the piece right-side out. With a finger or a blunt instrument, push the seams completely and smoothly outward (Fig. 10–37). Place the appliqué on the background fabric, lay a pressing sheet over it, and press (Fig. 10–38). The iron will melt the interfacing and affix the appliqué to the background making hand or machine stiching a breeze. This method is very handy but is best used for larger appliqués with smooth curves. It has a more prominent edge than other methods because of the added bulk of the interfacing.

Freezer-Paper Appliqué

This method uses freezer paper, found in most grocery stores, to hold the turned-under edges of the appliqué in place while it is hand stitched. Trace the template onto the paper side of the freezer paper (Fig. 10–39) and cut just inside the traced line. Place the freezer-paper shape on the wrong side of the fabric and cut it out about ¼" larger than the freezer paper (Fig. 10–40). Pre-trim and clip the fabric as shown on page 100. With the paper side of the freezer paper on the wrong side of the fabric, use the tip and side of an iron to fold and press the fabric to the edge of the freezer paper

Fig. 10–39

Fig. 10–40

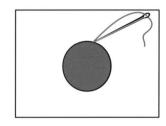

Fig. 10–41

(Fig. 10–41). Try not to touch the iron to the freezer paper. The thin layer of plastic on the freezer paper will melt and hold the fabric to the paper.

Iron the appliqué to the background fabric and hand appliqué (Fig. 10–42). If you appliqué with a sewing machine, it will be very difficult to remove the freezer paper at the end. You can remove the paper when you have just a little bit left to appliqué or you can appliqué around the entire shape, make a slit in the back just through the background fabric, and remove the paper through the slit. (Fig. 10–43) Close the slit with large, loose whip stitches or trim ¼" away from the stitching line and remove the background fabric and freezer paper.

Fig. 10–42

Gathered Appliqué

This method is helpful for making circles and oval shapes. Trace the template onto the back of the fabric. Cut out about ¼" outside the line (Fig. 10–44). Hand baste a line of loose running stitches between the traced line and the edge of the fabric, leaving several inches of thread tails at either end of the seam (Fig. 10–45). Place the template on the wrong side of the fabric (Fig. 10–46), pull the ends of the thread (Fig. 10–47), and gather the fabric around the template. Starch and press; remove the thread and the template. Sew the appliqué to the background by hand or machine (Fig. 10–48).

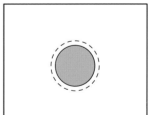

Fig. 10–43

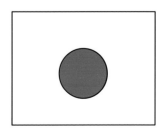

Fig. 10–48

Fig. 10–44   **Fig. 10–45**   **Fig. 10–46**   **Fig. 10–47**

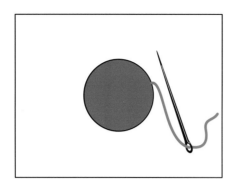

Fig. 10–49

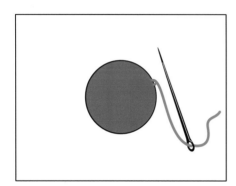

Fig. 10–50

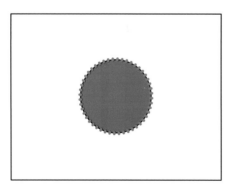

Fig. 10–51

Appliqué Stitching Methods

First, secure the appliqué to the background fabric. If using interfacing or freezer paper, place a pressing sheet over the appliqué and iron it to the background. If not, pin around the edges or use a few dabs of glue stick to secure the appliqué.

Hand Appliqué

Choose a thread that is the same color as the appliqué. Contrasting thread is shown on the illustrations for clarity. Knot the thread and push the needle up through the wrong side of the background fabric, catching 1–2 threads just on the outside edge of the appliqué (Fig. 10–49). Stitch straight down from the edge of the appliqué and into the background fabric. Come back up again ⅛"–¼" away from the first stitch (Fig. 10–50). Continue stitching around the appliqué. (Fig. 10–51) When done, take a small stitch behind the appliqué into the background fabric and thread the needle through the loop to make a knot.

Machine Appliqué

Choose a thread that blends well with the appliqué. Contrasting thread is shown on the illustration for clarity. Stitch around the edges with the sewing machine. Common stitches are the zigzag, blanket, and satin stitches.

For a zigzag stitch, use a fairly large width (3.5) and a short length (1). Adjust the sewing machine to see what different widths and lengths look like to determine which is best for the project.

Satin stitch is a tight zigzag. It has a large width, a shorter length of about 0.5, and it looks solid. It is a good choice for raw-edge appliqué as it covers the edge completely. It also gives the appliqué a strong outline.

The blanket stitch is sewn on the background fabric along the edge of the appliqué with a perpendicular stitch onto the appliquéd piece.

Tip

When machine appliquéing, one side of the stitch should land on the appliqué and the other side should be on the background fabric barely off the edge of the appliqué (Fig. 10–52). As you sew around the applique, make all adjustments to the fabric position with the needle down. This will prevent the fabric from slipping and having malformed stitches when you start sewing.

When sewing around a convex (outward) curve, leave the needle down in the background. To sew around a concave (inward) curve, adjust the fabric with the needle down in the applique fabric. This keeps the stitches tight together and not spread out. For points, stop with the needle down at the point of the fabric and rotate the fabric. The stitches at the point will overlap.

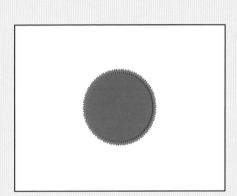

Fig. 10–52

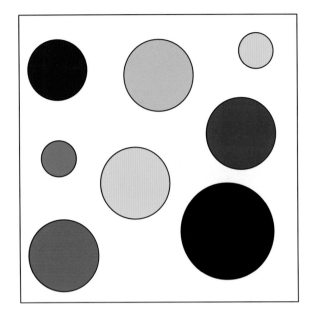

Circles Block

Templates

Prepare Circle Templates 1–4 (on the CD) by printing them onto cardstock or tracing them onto plastic. Cut them out on the outer, solid line. You may also make templates using a compass or by tracing circular household objects.

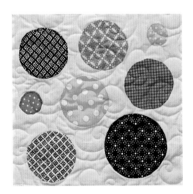

Fabrics

Choose assorted colors for the circles that will contrast with the background color.

Cutting and Tracing

Background fabric

Cut (1) 13½" x 13½" square

Circles

Trace assorted sizes of circles on the back of fabric using Templates 1–4

Cut

Rough cut around the circles, adding about an ¼"–½" seam allowance on all sides.

Assembly

The background square has been cut larger than the finished block size because appliqué work will often slightly shrink the background. Position the appliqués on the background leaving ample margins on the sides of the square to keep the appliqué edges from being sewn into the seam allowance when the block is trimmed to a 12½" x 12½" square.

Using the templates, make the appliqués. Arrange them into a pleasing design and then appliqué the circles to the background. Try the various finished-edge appliqué methods discussed on pages 100-105 to build your skills. Trim and square the block to 12½" x 12½" making sure to leave a ¼" seam allowance beyond the circles. You did it!

Tulip Cross Block

This beautiful appliquéd block provides an opportunity to apply all we have learned about appliqué so far, including making points. Referring to pages 100-105, use the appliqué methods you prefer.

Templates

Prepare Tulip Cross Templates 1–4 (on the CD) by printing them onto cardstock or tracing them onto plastic. Cut them out on the outer, solid line.

Fabrics

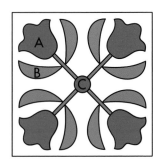

Fig. 10–53

Choose 3 colors to contrast with a background color (Fig. 10–53).

Cutting and Tracing

Before cutting the fabrics, determine the method you will use to appliqué them. For raw-edge appliqué, do not add seam allowances beyond the template shape. For finished-edge appliqué, cut the fabric about ¼"–½" larger than the template.

Background fabric
Cut (1) 13½" x 13½" square

Tulip flowers
Trace 4 copies of Template 1 onto Fabric A

Leaves
Trace 4 copies of Template 2 onto Fabric B
Turn Template 2 over and trace 4 reversed copies onto Fabric B

Center circle
Trace 1 copy of Template 3 onto Fabric C

Stems
Trace 2 copies of Template 4 onto Fabric B

Construction

Mark the diagonals of the background fabric with a removable marker (Fig. 10-54, page 108). The fabric is oversized so that any fraying due to handling can be trimmed off later. Trace the block layout with removable marker to ensure proper placement. You may wish to mark the 12" x 12" finished outline to make sure the appliqué stays

Fig. 10–54

within the block. If you are using an applique method that requires pressing, be sure to test on a scrap piece of fabric to make sure the removable marker is still removable after being pressed.

Trace the tulip cross pattern on the CD. Match the center dot on the pattern to the center of the X on the fabric. Transfer the pattern 4 times onto the background fabric (Fig. 10–55a and b). Include the outer, solid lines on the pattern to ensure the appliqués stay within the seam allowances.

Fig. 10–55a

Assembly

Appliqué the leaves into place. If you use a finished-edge appliqué method, there is no need to turn under the leaf ends at the stem because these will be covered by the stems. For raw-edge appliqué, the leaves may be placed over or under the stems. Complete the block by adding the stems, then the flowers, and finish with the center circle. Refer to the tip on page 100 for instructions on how to clip and trim the points of the leaves and flowers so they will turn under smoothly for finished-edge appliqué.

Center the block and then trim and square it to 12½" x 12½" making sure to leave a ¼" seam allowance beyond the appliqués. You did it!

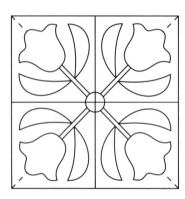

Fig. 10–55b

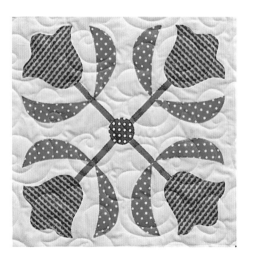

Skill Builder Set 11
Inset Seams

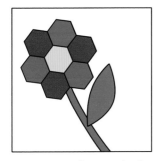

Hexagon Flower Block

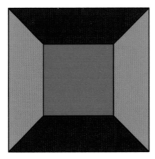

Mitered Frame Block

Mini Lone Star Block

nset or Y seams are used when three fabric pieces are sewn together and a simple straight seam won't do. With a bit of marking, pinning, and careful sewing, inset seams are not a problem.

We'll start with Hexagon Flower Block—a project you can take along anywhere since the hexagons are pieced by hand with a technique called English paper piecing.

For the next block, we will learn to make mitered borders. They may look difficult but are quite straightforward. Learning how to make a mitered border on a block will give you the skills to make a mitered border for a quilt.

Then we'll create a mini Lone Star, a popular pattern normally made as an entire quilt with many sets of diamonds. Using the same basic steps, you could easily expand the block to a larger project.

Hexagon Flower Block

nglish paper piecing is different from the foundation paper piecing. The fabric is basted around a removable paper template and then the fabric edges are whipstitched together to create the pattern. There are many ways to English paper piece; we will show our favorite. This method is also a great way to deal with shapes that require inset seams. It does mean sewing by hand, but English paper piecing is the perfect project to take to soccer games, the beach, or to work on while you are waiting for all those school concerts and assemblies to start.

We will use basic appliqué principles to make the stem and leaves for this block and to attach the fabric pieces onto the background fabric.

Templates

Prepare the Hexagon Flower Templates 1–4 on the CD by copying them onto cardstock or tracing them onto plastic. Cut them out on the outer line. Detailed information for making templates is on pages 77–78. These will be used to cut removable paper templates and fabric pieces.

Fabric

Choose 3 colors to contrast with a background color.

Cutting Paper Templates

Flower and center hexagons

Cut (7) of Template 1 without seam allowances from cardstock or freezer paper.

Leaves and stem

Cut 1 each of Templates 2–4 without seam allowances from cardstock or freezer paper.

Cutting and Tracing Fabric

Background

Cut (1) 13½" x 13½" square

Flower petals

Trace (6) of Template 1 on the back of fabric leaving at least ½" distance between each petal.

Flower center

Trace (1) of Template 1 on the back of fabric.

Left leaf

Trace (1) of Template 2 on the back of fabric.

Right leaf

Trace (1) of Template 3 on the back of fabric.

Stem

Trace (1) of Template 4 on the back of fabric.

Cut

Rough cut around the flower petals, center, leaves, and stem, adding about a ¼"–½" seam allowance on all sides.

Hexagon Basting Methods

There are three common ways to baste fabric around hexagons. Everyone who uses English paper piecing has their favorite. Leila prefers to baste the fabric to the paper templates by hand stitching through the paper for hexagons 1½" and smaller and to glue the edges on larger hexagons. Try out each method and see which you prefer. For all methods, hold the hexagon against the fabric. Rough cut around the template and add about a ¼"–½" seam allowance on all sides.

Method 1:
Basting Through the Templates
(Fig. 11–1)

This method is fast, secure, and the basting stitches are easy to remove. Some people object to damaging the templates by sewing through them, but they can be reused up to four times without losing their shape.

With a needle and thread (no need for a knot),

fold the fabric around one edge of the hexagon template and insert the needle through the paper and fabric about ¼" from a corner and pull the thread through, leaving a tail. Insert the needle again about ¼" from the other corner of the edge. Fold the next edge of fabric over the hexagon and stitch again. Repeat this for all six sides. Leave a thread tail at the end.

Method 2:

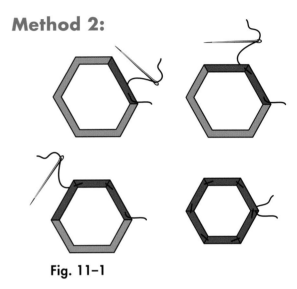

Fig. 11–1

Basting the Corners (Fig. 11–2)

This method uses stitches in the fabric at each hexagon corner to hold the fabric around the shape. It is best used with smaller hexagons; the fabric may not remain tight along the sides of larger hexagons. The advantage of this method is the paper templates can be removed without removing the basting stitches. Since the basting will not be removed, use a matching thread color that will not show on the right side of the fabric. To simplify removing the template, make a hole in the center of it and use a needle or other tool to pull it out when the basting is complete.

To baste the fabric at the corners, fold the fabric over two adjacent sides of the hexagon. Make a stitch under the fabric from one side of the corner to the other. Make a second stitch starting and ending in approximately the same place. These stitches will hold the fabric in place around the corner. Fold the fabric over the next side of the hexagon and stitch that corner. Continue all the way around the hexagon and leave a thread tail.

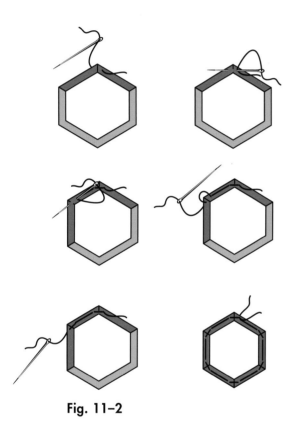

Fig. 11–2

Method 3:

Glue Basting (Fig. 11–3)

Place the paper template on the wrong side of the fabric and dab washable glue stick along one edge of the fabric. Fold the fabric over onto the paper. Repeat all the way around the template. After sewing the hexagons together, press the fabric with an iron to soften the glue and remove the paper. It is a bit more difficult to peel back the glue-basted fabric and a thin layer of the paper will often come off onto the fabric, but it is still a good method with larger hexagons.

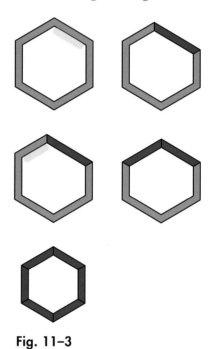

Fig. 11–3

Construction

Make 6 hexagons for the flower petals and 1 for the flower center using the basting method of your choice.

Lay out the hexagons (Fig. 11–4). Place the first 2 adjoining flower petal hexagons right sides together (Fig. 11–5). Choose a thread that blends with the fabrics, tie a knot in the end, and whipstitch the adjoining edges of fabric together.

To whipstitch (Fig. 11–6), insert the needle into the thin fold of fabric at the edge of the paper of both hexagons (a), pull the needle and thread through. Make the next stitch from the same side of the hexagon as the first stitch (b). Continue whipstitching until the hexagons are sewn together along one side (c). Be careful not to catch the paper with the needle as you stitch. Flatten out the two hexagons and make sure the stitches are not visible. If they are, the needle is catching too much fabric as you stitch.

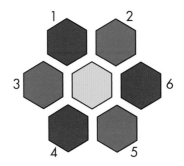

Fig. 11–4

With the same length of thread, whipstitch the center hexagon along one edge to the first petal (Fig. 11–7). Place the third flower petal to left of the center hexagon, whipstitch it to the hexagon above it (Fig. 11–8), and then tie off the thread. With a new knotted thread, stitch the third petal to the center, and then join the fourth petal to the lower edge of the third one above (Fig. 11–9). Tie off the thread, knot a new one, and stitch the fourth petal to the center hexagon, and continue whipstitching until the flower is complete (Fig. 11–10).

Fig. 11–5

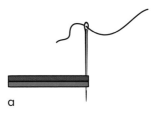

a

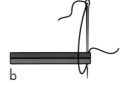

b

Create the leaves by turning the edges of the fabrics over one or two paper templates and basting them into place using one of the hexagon basting methods. Other appliqué methods of your choice can also be used. One leaf can be the mirror image of the other. Curves may require extra basting stitches to create a smooth curve. Create a stem by folding in the sides of the fabric so they meet in the middle or overlap until the stem is the width that you desire or use a ribbon or length of rickrack.

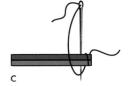

c

Fig. 11–6

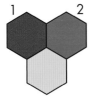

Fig. 11–7

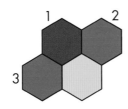

Fig. 11–8

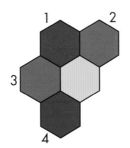

Fig. 11–9

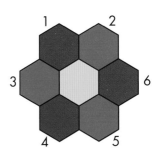

Fig. 11–10

Tip

If you want the stem to curve, you can use the distorting power of steam to your advantage. Prepare the stem by turning under the edges. Lay the stem on the ironing board and curve as desired. Set the iron at full steam and run it slowly over the stem. Give it an extra blast of steam from time to time. For tighter curves, cut the fabric on the bias at a 45° angle to the grain. This will help smooth the fabric.

Press the hexagons, leaves, and stem well. Remove the basting stitches and papers.

Assembly

Lay out all of the pieces within a 12" x 12" area in the center on the background fabric. Any appliqués beyond that area will disappear into the block's seam allowance. Use either a matching or a high-contrast thread to machine or hand stitch the leaves and stem onto the background block. Appliqué the hexagon flower onto the background making sure to cover the top of the stem with the petals.

Trim the block to 12½" x 12½", making sure to leave a ¼" seam allowance beyond the appliqués. You did it!

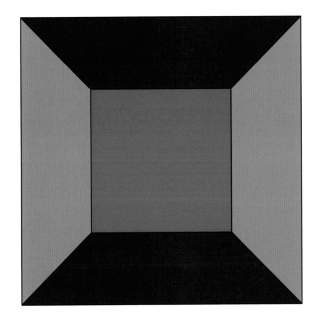

In order to make the border prints match in the mitered corners, there are some careful cutting procedures in addition to the following cutting instructions—the most important being the centering of the motif. Jinny's Perfect Piecer™ ruler helps to mark numerous common angles and the ¼" seam allowances for each or you can use your favorite rotary ruler.

Fabric

Choose 2 shades of the same color for the best 3-D effect and 1 contrasting color for the center to make the block shown above. Another option is to use 2 colors for the frame and a contrasting color for the center (Fig. 11–11a and 11–11b). This is a great opportunity to use a large print motif or even the Rosie poster print (Fig. 11–12) discussed on page 143.

Mitered Frame Block

Being able to make a mitered border is a great skill to have. You will use the same technique whether the mitered border is for a block, a pillow, or a quilt. We will show you how to make a fabric frame with regular printed fabric, but mitered borders can be even more stunning when they are made with striped fabric or symmetrical border-print fabrics, such as those designed by Jinny Beyer. Her fabrics are used to create designs that continue unbroken around the edges of a quilt.

Cutting

Center   Cut (1) 5¾" x 5¾" square.

Mitered frame   Cut (4) 13½" x 3⅞" rectangles—2 from one color and 2 from a shade of that color

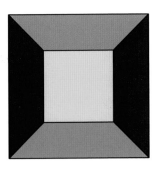

Fig. 11–11a

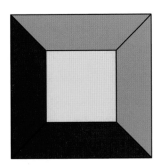

Fig. 11–11b

Fig. 11–12

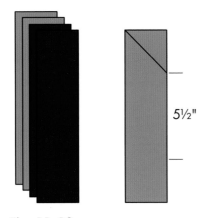

Fig. 11–13

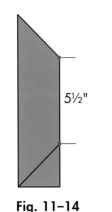

Fig. 11–14

Fig. 11–15

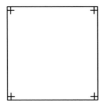

Fig. 11–16

Mitering 45° Angles

A 45° angle is used to miter the framed corners of squares and rectangles and is found on many rotary rulers; often there are (2) 45° angle lines that cross in the middle of the ruler, forming an X. These lines show you where to cut the angles needed to frame a four-sided project.

To miter, cut the rectangles for the Mitered Frame block, neatly stack them right-side up matching all of the edges. Cutting them together will ensure they are all the exact same size, but you must be accurate. Measure twice, cut once! Place one of the 45° angle lines of a ruler on the left edge of the fabric to be mitered. This will rotate the edge of the ruler diagonally across the stack of fabric rectangles at a 45° angle. Before cutting the miter, look closely at Fig. 11–13 to make sure that angle of the ruler's edge will make the cut in the same direction as shown in the diagram. If not, turn the ruler a quarter turn at a time until the angle matches the diagram and then trim the corner off.

Measure 5½" from the lower edge of the diagonal cut and make a tiny mark on the right edge of the fabric. Place the 45° angle line of the ruler on the lower left edge of the fabric and position the ruler so its diagonal edge goes from the left edge of the fabric to the 5½" mark made on the right edge. If it does not, turn the ruler a quarter turn until the angle is correct. Look closely at Fig. 11–14 to make sure that the cut matches the diagram and then trim the end off. The resulting shape is a trapezoid (Fig. 11–15).

Construction

Use a Perfect Piecer or a rotary ruler to mark the ¼" seam allowances on the back of the fabric at each corner of the center square. Place the ¼" line of the ruler on the edge of the fabric at one corner and draw a short faint line to mark about ½" of the end of the seam allowance. Place the ruler on the other side of the corner with the ¼" line of the ruler on the edge of the fabric and draw another short faint line that intersects with the first one to form an X (Fig. 11–16). Mark all 4 corners with an X. Mark the corners of the trapezoid in the same manner as the center square (Fig. 11–17)

Fig. 11–17

Since the marks were made on the outer side of the ruler, the true ¼" intersection is just on the inside of the X (Fig. 11–18). This is where the needle should start and stop for this type of seam. The inner edges of the trapezoid are ¼" smaller than the edges of the center square. This allows the ¼" seam intersections and fabric edges to match. The corners will not match perfectly but they are in the seam allowance and do not affect the construction of the block.

Fig. 11–18

To match the intersections of the inner edge of a trapezoid and one side of the center square, place them right sides together. Insert a pin through the back of the fabric through one of the intersections. If the pin comes out at the intersection on the other side, the 2 pieces are aligned correctly. If not, adjust the fabric and pins until they are. Place the needle in the first intersection and, with a locked stitch, sew the pieces right sides together. Stop at the opposite marked intersection and lock the stitch. Do not stitch past the intersection (Fig. 11–19).

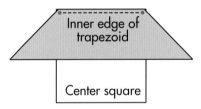

Fig. 11–19

Sew another trapezoid to the center square. Fold back the corner of the previous trapezoid so that it does not get sewn into the seam allowance. Sew all 4 trapezoids to the center square. Fold the center block on the diagonal with right sides together. Match and pin 2 of the mitered trapezoid edges together at the intersections marked on the back of the fabric. Sew the seam (Fig. 11–20). Repeat and sew the remaining 3 corners. Press the center square seam toward the frame. Press the mitered seams in the frame whichever direction they want to go. You did it! Center a ruler on the block to make sure it is 12½" x 12½".

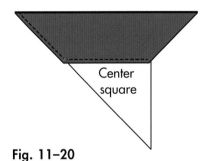

Fig. 11–20

Mini Lone Star Block

Strip piecing and cutting at a 45° angle creates the appearance of diamonds pieced in a row. Using the basic concepts to make the Mini Lone Star block, you can make any size Lone Star block or quilt.

Fabric

Choose 3 colors—a light, a dark, and a medium for the diamonds—to contrast with a background color.

Cutting

Light fabric	Cut (1) 1¾" x 23" strip
Medium fabric	Cut (2) 1¾" x 23" strips
Dark fabric	Cut (1) 1¾" x 23" strip
Background	Cut (4) 4" x 4" squares
	Cut (1) 6¼" x 6¼" square

Cut the 6½" x 6½" square in half diagonally in both directions.

> **Tip**
> Cutting diamond units from strip-sets is the perfect technique for making accurate Lone Stars.

Construction

Sew the light strip to a medium strip and the dark strip to the remaining medium strip, each with a scant ¼" seam. Press the seams toward the light and dark strips. The strip-sets should now be 3" x 23". Place the 45° line of a rotary ruler along the length of a strip-set (Fig. 11–21). Trim the end of the strip at a 45° angle.

Place the 1¾" line of a ruler along the trimmed diagonal end of the strip-set (Fig. 11–22) and cut to make a diamond unit. Cut 8 diamond units from each strip-set for a total of 16 diamond units. Press all of the seam allowances in the same direction.

Lay out and pair the diamond units from one strip-set with a diamond unit from the

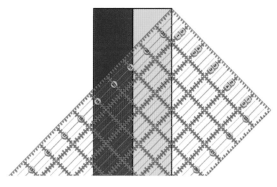

Fig. 11–21

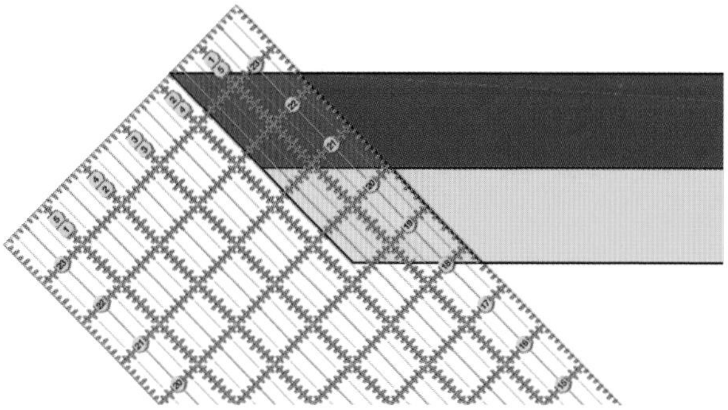

Fig. 11–22

other strip-set (Fig. 11–23) for a total of 8 pairs. It is important that the colors are in the same position for all of the pairs. Place a pair of diamond units right sides together. The seams will not nest together but will intersect diagonally ¼" from the edge along the seam line (Fig. 11–24). Match the point of the intersections on both diamond units together with pins. Sew a scant ¼" seam to join the 2 diamond units to create a four-patch diamond unit (Fig. 11–25). Make 8 four-patch diamond units. Press the seams all in the same direction.

Fig. 11–23

Check to make sure all of the diamond units look the same; each should have a light diamond at one end and a dark diamond at the other. Mark the ¼" seam intersections on all of the outer points of the four-patch diamond units (Fig. 11–26). Mark the ¼" seam intersections on 3 corners of each 4" x 4" background square and on all 3 corners of the background triangles. Lay out the diamond units with the background triangles at the sides and the squares at each corner (Fig. 11–27, page 120).

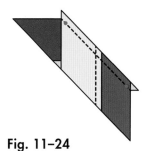

Fig. 11–24

Assembly

Matching the seam intersections, sew 2 four-patch diamond units together (Fig. 11–28, page 120), locking the stitches at each start and stop intersection. Do not sew past the intersection to the edge of the fabric. Continue joining the diamond units until you have all 8 sewn together for the center of the block. Press the seams all in the same direction. If you haven't stitched past the marked intersections, the seams at the center of the block should fan out easily.

Fig. 11–25

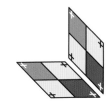

Fig. 11–26

■ Inset Seams ■
■ Mini Lone Star Block ■

Fig. 11–27

Fig. 11–28

Fig. 11–29

Fig. 11–30

Next, add the side triangles. Match and pin the ¼" marked intersections on left side of a triangle with the marked intersections on the right side of a four-patch diamond unit. Begin sewing at the marked outer intersection, lock the stitch, and sew to the marked intersection at the inner point of the triangle (Fig. 11–29 shows the stitches from the right side of the block.) Lock the stitches and, with the needle down, pivot the fabric. Match and pin the marked intersection on the right side of the triangle with the marked intersection near the tip of the diamond unit on the right. Stitch to the intersection and then lock and cut the stitches (Fig. 11–30 shows the stitches from the back of the block.)

Sew all of the triangles between the four-patch diamond units (Fig. 11–31). Add the corner squares in the same way (Fig. 11–29). Center a ruler on the block and then trim and square it to 12½" x 12½", making sure to leave a ¼" seam allowance beyond the diamond points. Whew! You did it!

Fig. 11–31

Tip

If you find that the pieced bias-edged diamond units end up a bit bigger than the accurately cut squares or triangles, put the diamonds on the bottom when you sew them to the squares and triangles. This will help ease in the extra fabric on the diamonds and make the edges match.

Skill Builder Set 12
Challenge Blocks—You Can Do It!

Compass Block

Feathered Star Block

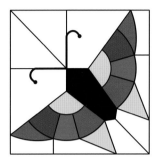

Butterfly Block

We are not going to lie to you. The blocks in this chapter are very challenging. Each will incorporate in one block many of the skills you have learned. They are time-consuming and require precise piecing, but you can totally do it. And when you do, you are going to be so proud! We want you to carry around your blocks for the next few days and show them to everyone. You are an amazing quilter!

Compass Block

This is the type of block that looks impossible to piece, but all it really takes is time and perseverance. Paper piecing makes those sharp points come out perfectly. The major differences between this foundation-pieced block and the ones you made in Skill Builder Set 7 are that this one is pieced in eighths, has 2 different foundations used to make the block, and there are a lot of points to match. Careful labeling

of the fabric and foundations, and basting the sections together before doing the final seams, make those challenges are surmountable.

Foundations

Make 4 copies each of Compass Foundation A and Foundation B on the CD. Confirm the length of the 2 outer triangle sides are each 6". The length of the diagonal side is 8½". The solid lines are to be sewn on and the outer dashed line is the trim line to use after the foundation has been pieced. Detailed information on making foundations is found on pages 64–65.

The combination of Foundations A and B make ¼ of the block (Fig. 12–1). The longest and most forward spike (reds B & C) is split between the 2 foundations. The middle spike (teals D & E) is also split between Foundations A and B. The spike in the background (yellows F & G) is not split on either foundation (Fig. 12–2).

Fabric

Choose 2 shades each of 3 colors that will contrast with a background color.

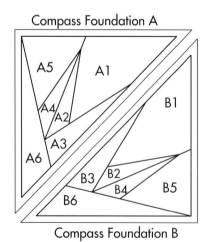

Compass Foundation A

Compass Foundation B

Fig. 12–1

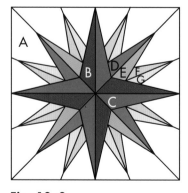

Fig. 12–2

Tip

As the fabric is cut, pin a piece of paper labeled with a foundation letter and a section number to each set of fabrics. There are so many sections and fabrics that this step is essential. An extra way to ensure each fabric gets sewn in the correct section is to write the name or color of each fabric in its appropriate section on the foundations. Remember that the foundation is a mirror image of the final block and label accordingly.

Cutting

The alpha-numeric following the each cut represents the foundation and the section to which the fabric will be sewn.

Fabric A (background)
Cut (4) 6½" x 6½" squares cut once on the diagonal (A1)
Cut (4) 3½" x 5" rectangles (A5)
Cut (4) 4" x 3½" rectangles (B1)
Cut (4) 5½" x 5" rectangles (B4)

Fabric B (dark red)
Cut (4) 7½" x 2½" rectangles (B6)

Fabric C (light red)
Cut (4) 7½" x 2½" rectangles (A6)

Fabric D (dark teal)
Cut (4) 2" x 5" rectangles (A3)

Fabric E (light teal)
Cut (4) 2" x 5" rectangles (B5)

Fabric F (dark yellow)
Cut (8) 1½" x 4¼" rectangles (A4, B3)

Fabric G (light yellow)
Cut (8) 1½" x 4¼" rectangles (A2, B2)

Construction

The same methods described in Skill Builder Set 7 (pages 64-65) are used to create this block. (Refer to Figs. 12–1 and 12–2 for color placement.) Begin with Foundation A and place the A1 fabric face up on the unmarked back of the foundation. Pin or glue the fabric into place. Using a piece of cardstock, fold the foundation back on the line between sections 1 and 2.

Trim the fabric ¼" from the fold. Unfold the foundation and place the A2 fabric right sides together along the trimmed edge of A1. Take care that the fabrics are lined up correctly and will cover all of the compass points when flipped open. Since the points are so narrow, much of the point can hide in the seam allowance making it difficult to see where it begins and ends.

Decrease the stitch length to 18–20 stitches per inch. Flip the foundation over and sew on the line between section 1 and 2. Continue adding fabric in numerical order in this manner until the foundation is complete. As the foundations are pieced, you will see impressive points form. Pay special attention while pressing. If the seams are not pressed completely open, the points will not look like they meet correctly. Trim the foundations ¼" from the solid inner line.

Repeat these steps for Foundation B.

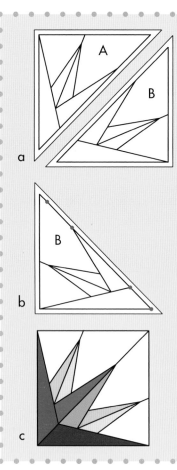

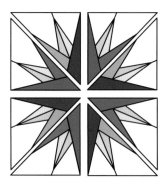

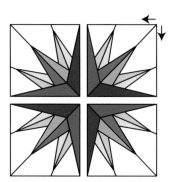

Tip

Here are some tricks to make sure the points meet perfectly (Fig. 12–3). Verify that the foundations are lined up correctly (a). Pin Foundations A and B together at the beginning and end of the diagonal seam and at each of the points. Lower the sewing machine needle into the sewing line to make a needle hole through the foundations; then lift the needle and remove the foundations. If the needle came out on exactly on the sewing line on the lower foundation, the foundations are aligned correctly.

Machine baste the foundations together (b). Increase the stitch length to between 3 and 4 and take 5–10 basting stitches at the beginning and the end of the seam and at each point. Open the foundations and check to see if the points meet correctly (c). If they don't, it is easy to remove the stitches, adjust the foundations, and baste again. Once they are basted correctly, reduce the stitch length and sew over the basting, as normal.

LEFT: **Figs. 12–3a, b, and c**

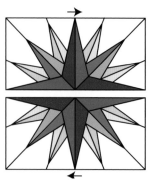

Fig. 12–4

Assembly

Lay out the foundations (Fig. 12–4) and sew Foundations A and B together along the diagonal (Fig. 12–5). We usually recommend pressing seams to one side or the other; however, because of the fabric bulk at the points, pressing them open may be a better option. Sew the 4 quarters together (Fig. 12–6) to finish the block (Fig. 12–7). Remember to baste and check the points as you go. You did it! Make sure the block measures 12½" x 12½".

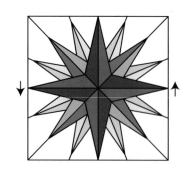

Fig. 12–5

Fig. 12–6

Fig. 12–7

Foundations

Print 4 copies each of Feathered Star Foundations A–D on the CD. Write the fabric name or color on each foundation section with pen or pencil; it is very easy to get confused with so many small pieces (Fig. 12–8). The solid lines are to be sewn on and the outer dashed line is the trim line to use after the foundation has been pieced.

Fabric

Choose 1 color each for the star, the feathers, and the background.

Feathered Star Block

This intricate block is made easier by paper piecing. It is challenging and time intensive but the finished block is worth the effort. We are introducing a new technique with this block—partial seams. With these, an inch or so of the seam is left unstitched and then finished after other pieces have been attached. Using partial seams avoids multiple inset seams.

Cutting

The alpha-numeric following each cut represents the foundation and the section to which the fabric will be sewn.

Background fabric

(20) 2¼" x 2¼" squares cut once on the diagonal (A2, A4, B1, B4, B7, C2, C6, D2, D4)

(4) 4½" x 4½" squares (A4)

(1) 8" x 8" square cut on both diagonals (C7)

Star fabric

(4) 3½" x 3½" squares cut once on the diagonal (B6, D5)

(1) 4⁵⁄₁₆" x 4⁵⁄₁₆" square. The ⁵⁄₁₆" mark is between the ⅜" and ¼" marks

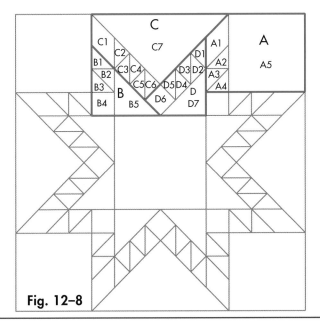

Fig. 12–8

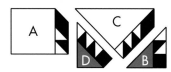

Fig. 12–9

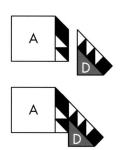

Fig. 12–10

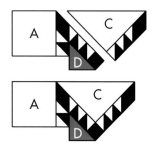

Fig. 12–11

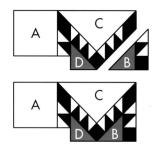

Fig. 12–12

Fig. 12–13

Feather fabric

- (8) 2" x 3" rectangles (A1, C1)

- (14) 2¼" x 2¼" squares cut once on the diagonal (B3, B5, D3)

- (8) 1¾" x 1¾" squares (D1, B1)

Construction

Place the first piece of fabric face up on the unmarked back of a foundation. Pin or glue it in place. Using cardstock, fold the foundation back on the line between sections 1 and 2. Trim the fabric ¼" from the fold. Unfold the foundation and place the second fabric right sides together along the trimmed edge. Take care that the fabrics are lined up correctly and will cover the compass points when flipped open. Since the points are so narrow, much of the point can hide in the seam allowance making it difficult to see where it begins and ends.

Decrease the stitch length to 18–20 stitches per inch. Flip the foundation over and sew on the line between section 1 and 2. Continue adding fabric in numerical order in this manner until the foundation is complete. Pay special attention while pressing. If the seams are not pressed completely open, the points will not look like they meet correctly. Trim the foundations ¼" from the solid inner line.

Assembly

Lay out 1 each of Foundations A, B, C, and D as a unit (Fig. 12–9). Sew Foundation A to Foundation D (Fig. 12–10). A will not reach the bottom of D. Start sewing at the top and end about ½"–¾" before the end of foundation A. This is the first of the partial seams. Sew Foundation C to the AD unit along the entire length of the seam (Fig. 12–11). Sew Foundation B to the ADC unit (Fig. 12–12). Make (4) ABCD units. We will call these feather units.

Arrange the feather units around the center square (Fig. 12–13). It is not possible to sew all the units together in straight lines across the block. This is where partial seams work to finish the piecing. Sew the center square to the DB side of one of the feather units (Fig. 12–14). Match the left edge of the square to the left edge of D, sew, and then stop about 1" before the end of the center square. Add the next feather unit by sewing its BC side to the A side of the previous unit (Fig. 12–15). Having a partial seam between Foundations A and D allowed this feather unit to be sewn on, and now that it has been, it is time to finish the seam (Fig. 12–16). Begin sewing about ½" before the partial seam ended between Foundation A and D and stitch to the end of the center square.

Repeat the steps in the paragraph above to join the remaining feather units around the center square. Sew the third feather unit to the block (Fig. 12–17) and then sew the last unit to the block (Fig. 12–18). Close the last partial seam, stitching ½" into the previous seams at either end (Fig. 12–19). Remove the paper after the block is sewn into the quilt by carefully folding each seam line and tearing the paper away. Check to make sure the block is 12½" x 12½" square. You did it! You finished a killer of a block. Give yourself a pat on the back and show the block to all of your friends. You are an amazing quilter and can piece anything!

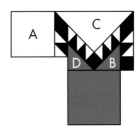

Fig. 12–14

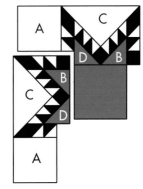

Fig. 12–15

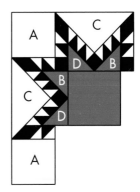

Fig. 12–16

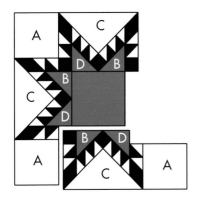

Fig. 12–17

Fig. 12–18

Fig. 12–19

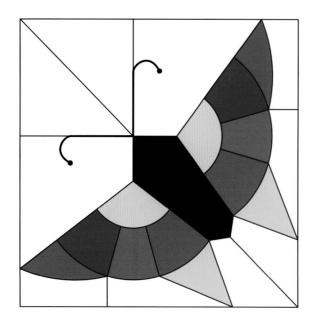

Butterfly Block

According to Jinny Beyer in her book, *The Quilter's Album of Patchwork Patterns*, (Breckling Press, 2009), this block was originally designed by Laura Wheeler and published in 1937 in the *Minneapolis Star*. It has been modified slightly from the original (the triangles in the upper left corner were redrawn to have right angles) to simplify the cutting and piecing. However, because of the curves and inset seams, it will still be a challenge. Review Skill Builder Set 8—Curves and Skill Builder Set 11—Inset Seams, if necessary.

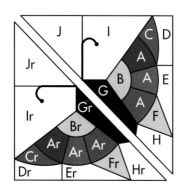

Fig. 12–20

Templates

Prepare the Butterfly Templates A–J on the CD by printing them onto cardstock or tracing them onto plastic. Cut them out on the outer line. This block is the mirror image of itself along the diagonal so the same templates can be used for both sides if the pieces for one side are traced and cut with the template facing up and the pieces for the other side are traced and cut with the templates facing down.

Tip

A quick way to cut a piece and its reverse image is to fold the fabric right sides together, trace the template onto the top layer, and then cut through both layers. To make it even quicker, use a mini-rotary cutter to cut around the template. Just be sure the fabric doesn't slip while using either method or the pieces might not be accurate. Be sure to label the pieces as they are cut to avoid confusion during piecing.

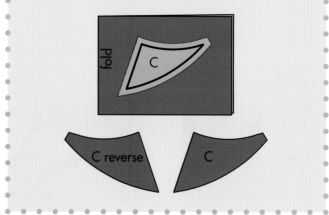

Fabric

Choose a variety of colors and a contrasting background color.

Cutting

Template A

Cut 3 pieces face up and 3 pieces
face down.

Templates B–J

Cut 1 piece each face up and 1 piece each
face down.

Fig. 12–21

Fig. 12–22

Fig. 12–23

Construction

Sew (3) A pieces together into an arc (Fig. 12–21). Make (2) A units. Find the center of the A units and the B pieces. Match the centers and pin (Fig. 12–22). Pin at the corners (Fig. 12–23) and carefully sew them together (Fig. 12–24).

Sew C and D together. D is almost symmetrical, but one side is a little thicker than the other. Place the wider-angled end of C on the thicker end of D. Pin at the center (Fig. 12–25) and then at the ends (Fig. 12–26) and ease the fabric between the pins. Sew the curve between C and D (Fig. 12–27). Repeat these steps to make the reversed CD unit. Sew F to E and then attach the CD and EF units together. Repeat these steps to make the reverse CDEF unit (Fig. 12–28). Fold the AB and the CDEF units in half to find the centers of the curves. Match the center of the AB unit with the center of the CDEF. Pin the units together along the length of the curve and sew. Repeat these steps for the reverse ABCDEF unit (Fig. 12–29).

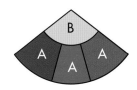

Fig. 12–24

Fig. 12–25   **Fig. 12–26**

Fig. 12–27

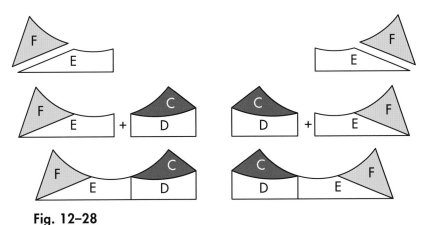

Fig. 12–28

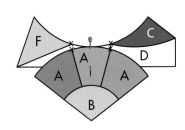

Fig. 12–29

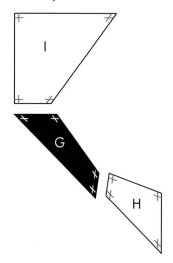

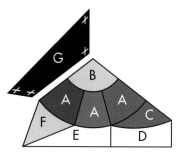

Fig. 12–30

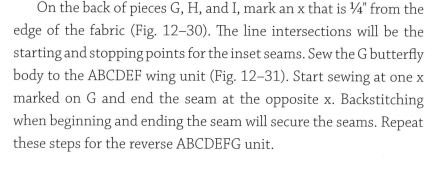

On the back of pieces G, H, and I, mark an x that is ¼" from the edge of the fabric (Fig. 12–30). The line intersections will be the starting and stopping points for the inset seams. Sew the G butterfly body to the ABCDEF wing unit (Fig. 12–31). Start sewing at one x marked on G and end the seam at the opposite x. Backstitching when beginning and ending the seam will secure the seams. Repeat these steps for the reverse ABCDEFG unit.

Sew H in place by carefully matching the intersection of the x on H with the x on G. Pin and sew from the x outward to the sides (Fig. 12–32). Use the same steps to attach I to the top of the butterfly. Repeat these steps to sew the reverse H and I to the reverse unit. Sew J to the unit to complete it (Fig. 12–33) and then complete the reverse unit. If necessary, trim along the diagonal to straighten triangle. Sew the halves together matching the seams at the top and bottom of the body unit and press the seams. Follow the seam line between I and J to sketch the antennae. Sew on the line with a narrow satin stitch or hand stitch with embroidery floss.

Check to make sure the block measures 12½" x 12½". You did it!

Fig. 12–31

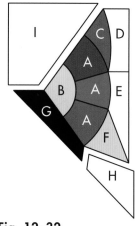

Fig. 12–32

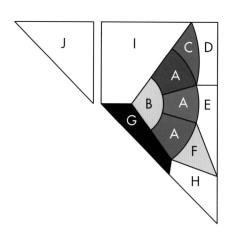

Fig. 12–33

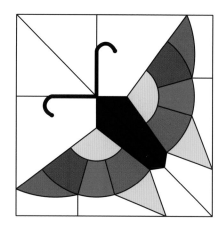

Fig. 12–34

Skill Builder Set 13
Finishing the You Can Do It! Skill Builder Quilt

n this chapter we provide directions for making a quilt from the blocks you have made. You can find additional quilt layout suggestions for making several smaller quilts with the blocks on Marlene's website (www.kissedquilts.com).

There are many different ways to arrange your blocks. You could have the quilt change in coloration from top to bottom or corner to corner or place the blocks to ensure that the various fabrics are sprinkled evenly across the quilt. You can arrange the quilt blocks in numerical order so you can see your skill building progression or mix them up so the different styles of blocks are found throughout the quilt. It's up to you.

When cutting sashings and borders, it is best to cut them on the length of the fabric. The direction of the grain of the fabric helps to keep your quilt squared up. The material requirements are enough so that you can cut them on the length of fabric. Less fabric may be needed if you choose to cut them on the cross grain (across the width) of the fabric and piece them together. Do not cut the border strips until you have measured your quilt so you can adjust the border lengths if necessary.

All of the given measurements assume that all of your blocks have squared up to 12½" x 12½", which will result in a 12" x 12" finished block after assembled into the quilt top. Border dimensions are based on maintaining expected finished sizes throughout assembly. However, that assumption is a bit optimistic. Small variations in seam width can add up over the course of making the quilt and it is always a good idea to measure the quilt top after the blocks are sewn together before cutting the borders. Measure vertically through the middle and along the sides for the side borders. Measure across the top, middle, and bottom for the top and bottom borders. If your vertical or horizontal measurements are not consistent, average them. Cut the borders opposite each other the same length and make the edges of the quilt top fit when sewing the borders on. This will help keep the quilt square.

Tip
Remember to set your seams by pressing the seam with the fabric right sides together before pressing open. This will help keep those long seams straight and your quilt square.

Assembling the Top

Fabric

(36) 12½" x 12½" unfinished quilt blocks from the Skill Builder Sets

Finishing fabrics and batting listed on page 8.

Cutting

Sashing: Double-check that your blocks measure 12½" x 12½" before cutting.

Cut (5) 12½" x the remaining width of fabric strips, subcut into (60) 2½" x 12½" rectangles

Cornerstones

Cut (2) 2½" x width of fabric strips, subcut into (25) 2½" x 2½" squares

You can also use scraps from a variety of fabrics to cut the cornerstones.

> **Tip**
>
> Measure your quilt top before cutting the borders to make sure the measurements match. Adjust the lengths as needed.

Inner borders

Cut (2) 2½" x 82½" strips cut lengthwise

Cut (2) 2½" x 86½" strips cut lengthwise

Outer borders

Cut (2) 86½" x 6½" strips cut lengthwise

Cut (2) 98½" x 6½" strips cut lengthwise

Note

Binding instructions start on page 135.

Assembly

Lay out the sashings, cornerstones, and blocks based on the layout diagram (page 132). Sew rows of sashings and cornerstones and rows of blocks and sashings. Press the seam allowances toward the sashing strips. Sew the rows together, matching the seams. Press toward the sashing strips.

Measure to check quilt center dimensions and cut the inner side borders accordingly. Sew them onto each side. Press toward the border.

Measure to check quilt center and cut the top and bottom inner border accordingly. Sew them to the top and bottom.

Add the outer borders using the same method. Press toward the borders.

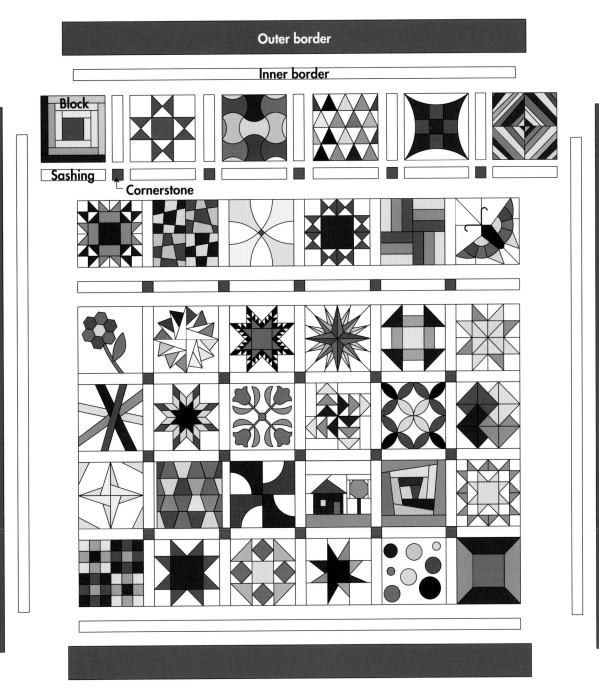

Quilt layout diagram, 98" x 98"

Quilting

A warm cover is simply a blanket unless there are three parts—a top, batting, and a backing. This makes up the *quilt sandwich*. You've pieced the blocks together and assembled them into a top. Now you are ready to assemble the sandwich and quilt it.

Consider if you want to quilt it yourself by hand, on a home machine, or take it to a professional quilter. Be sure to check with the quilter about their specific requirements and consider these general suggestions when making quilting decisions and fabric purchases. The batting and backing may be available directly from the professional and must typically be at least 4"–8" larger than the top in each direction. The professional will load all 3 pieces (top, batting, and backing) separately onto their quilting equipment, so do not sandwich them together.

Here are some basic guidelines for sandwiching a quilt to be done by hand or on your own machine.

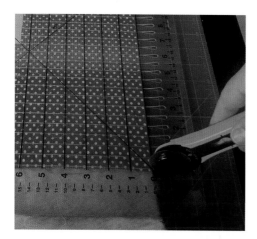

Fig. 13–1

> ### Tip
> Spray basting is an alternative to pin basting. Follow the spray manufacturer's instructions.

Lay out the backing right-side down on the floor or a table and use pins or painter's tape to anchor it. The backing should be smooth and taut, but not tight. Layer the batting on top of the backing. Smooth it from the center outward to each edge. Use painter's tape in a few spots to keep the batting taut. Lay the quilt top on top of the batting. Smooth it from center outward to each edge.

Insert safety pins (bent quilter's safety pins work easiest) evenly across the quilt or hand baste the three layers together. Consider where you will quilt and pin accordingly to minimize pin removal during the quilting process.

Quilting is the stitching that holds the three layers together and quilting possibilities are endless. Different feet are used depending on the type of quilting. Use a walking foot to get great straight-line quilting. Free-motion quilting requires the use of a "darning" or "quilting" foot.

Consider the motif of the fabric, purpose of the quilt, and meaningful words or statistics to give you ideas on how to quilt it. Quilt as desired. You could continue the sampler theme presented in this book and try a different quilting style on each block. After quilting, trim of the extra batting and backing around all sides of the entire sandwich. Measure against the border seams to straighten the quilt and check that corners are square (Fig. 13–1).

Binding

Traditional bindings are double-folded and applied by machine to the front of the quilt and wrapped to the back to be stitched down by hand. The thickness of the batting may determine how wide to make the binding; most are cut 2½" wide. If using a thin batting and applying the binding completely by machine, 2¼" is sufficient and keeps the binding narrow. To bind rounded corners or scalloped edges, cut the binding on the bias.

Measure the length of all sides of the quilt. Add them together and divide by 40, the typical width of fabric and round up to a whole number (i.e. 10.3 = 11). If it was close, you may want to cut an extra binding strip, just in case. Cut the number of strips you need and sew them end to end on the diagonal (Fig. 13–2). Trim and press each seam (Fig. 13–3). Cut one end of the binding strip at a 45° angle. We will start sewing at the end. Fold the binding in half lengthwise with wrong sides together and press.

Align the raw edge of the binding with the trimmed edge of the quilt sandwich. If finishing the binding by hand, apply the binding by machine to the front of the quilt. To do a complete binding by machine, start on the back of the quilt (Fig. 13 –4). Avoid positioning a binding seam intersection at the corners of the quilt. Adjust the diagonally cut starting point of the binding accordingly and check the quilt corners again.

To determine the width of the seam allowance for the binding, insert a pin into the binding parallel to the quilt's edge and about ¼"–⅜" from the raw edge. Fold the binding over the pin and around the edge of the quilt to test if the binding will cover the seam line (where the pin is). Adjust the width the seam allowance until you like how the binding looks.

Fig. 13–2

Fig. 13–3

Fig. 13–4

Fig. 13–5

Fig. 13–6

Fig. 13–7

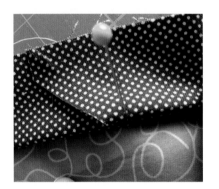

Fig. 13–8

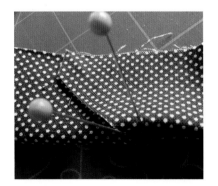

Fig. 13–9

A walking foot is recommended for stitching the binding onto the quilt. Some machines have them built-in; others may need to have the foot changed. Begin sewing about 12" from the diagonal end. Stitch about 4" and lock the stitch. Remove the quilt from the machine and place a stop pin about 12" to the left of the starting point. This pin marks the point to stop sewing the binding to the quilt so there will be sufficient room to stitch the binding ends together.

Test the binding again to make sure it covers the seam line on the other side of the quilt. If you are happy with the alignment, continue stitching. When you are the same distance from the edge of the quilt as the width of the seam, stop with the needle in the down position, pivot the quilt, and stitch diagonally into the corner (Fig. 13 –5). This time, stop with the needle up and move the quilt a few inches away from the needle but do not cut the threads. Rotate the quilt to get ready to stitch along the next edge.

The binding must be folded carefully to make a nice mitered corner. There are other methods of doing this, but this is one we have found to be simple and effective for utility quilts. Diagonally fold the binding back upon itself toward the top of the quilt and along the short diagonal seam in the corner to make a 45° fold in the binding (Fig. 13–6). Holding the diagonal fold in place, fold the binding again downward along the unsewn edge of the quilt, matching the raw edges (Fig. 13–7). Make sure the second fold is flush with the top of the quilt.

Place the quilt back under the needle holding the still-attached threads to keep them from tangling and sew, beginning at the corner and with the same seam allowance, along the new edge of the quilt. Continue around the quilt folding the remaining corners until you reach the stop pin. Remove the quilt from the sewing machine.

Align the binding ends one on top of the other so they overlap. Insert a pin through both binding strips ¼" from the diagonally cut edge of the binding (Fig. 13-8). Insert two more pins at the same point with one pin through one binding strip and the other pin through the other strip (Fig. 13–9). Turn the binding edges right sides together on the diagonal, align the two strips at the pin points (Fig. 13–10, page 136), and sew them together. Before trimming, make sure the length of the binding is correct for the remaining area of the quilt to be stitched. Adjust the seam if necessary. Trim the seam, align the raw edges, and stitch the binding to the quilt.

To finish binding by hand, fold the binding to the back and use a slip stitch to attach it to the quilt back. To finish by machine, turn the binding to the front of the quilt and topstitch on the folded edge of the binding (Fig. 13–11). As you approach each corner, fold the next edge in (Fig. 13–12) and wrap the current edge over the top. This allows the mitered fold to be the opposite of the fold on the other side of the quilt. Finish sewing the binding (Fig. 13–13) and then lock the stitches.

Labeling

No matter the intended use of the quilt, we recommend that you label it. As it is passed down through generations, let the story be known of its origin. Labels are traditionally applied to the lower left corner of the quilt when you're facing the back of the quilt. There are many ways that labels can be made: writing on the back with a permanent fabric pen (not a Sharpie®), writing on a separate piece of fabric, or printing on treated fabric and sewing or fusing either to the back of the quilt; embroidering a label and attaching it.

Information to consider including:
The name of the quilt
The name of the quilt top maker
The name of the quilter, if different
Location of its creation
The date the quilt was completed, especially if it's for a special occasion or purpose
A saying or appropriate words for the occasion of the gift or the reason for its creation

Once the label is attached, you can truly say, I Did It!

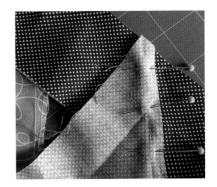

Fig. 13–10

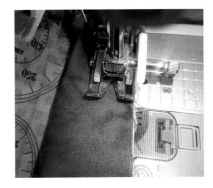

Fig. 13–11

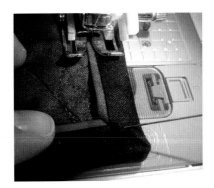

Fig. 13–12

Fig. 13–13

FRAMED, 70" x 84½".

Pieced by Kate Challis, Leila Gardunia, Amy Martin, Jill McBroom, Sara McDaniel,
Julie Schloemer, and Emma Thomas McGinnis. Quilted by Leila Gardunia.
Instructions for this alternate finishing method can be found on the CD along with a
gallery of other quilt finishing options.

Acknowledgments

Thank you to Moda for providing fabric for several of the quilts.

A great big thank you to Leila's block testers Kate Challis, Amy Martin, Jill McBroom, Sara McDaniel, Julie Schloemer, and Emma Thomas-McGinnis. Your help was invaluable!

Another huge thank you goes to Marlene's first Skill Builder class which reviewed a number of the drafted chapters and helped us understand how many different types of learners there are.

From Leila

This book would never have been written without the day-to-day support and encouragement of my husband Brian. Words cannot express how grateful I am for his love and sacrifice.

Thank you to Sandi Walton who blogs at Piecemeal Quilts—your posts caused me to examine my quilting goals and made me realize I hadn't been stretching myself to my full quilting potential. I would never have started this journey without your inspiration.

And, without Marlene, the journey would never have ended with a book. Thank you!

From Marlene

When I let God lead in my life, doors opened for my quilting adventure and I am so grateful. Marrying Duncan, who encourages me to pursue my passion rather than a career, has been an exciting path to explore. Thanks, Lover!

Thank you to Leila for using the Rosie the Riveter poster for her quilt-along blog button. This initially drew me into the project; I wanted to incorporate the poster into my quilt. I learned many piecing skills and experimented with a variety of quilting styles.

I am also grateful to Leila for meeting me that important day at AQS Quilt Week® Des Moines where my quilt, Rosie's BOMb, won second place in the Bed Quilts, Machine Quilted category and we decided to work on this book together. The quilt has won several ribbons in local, regional, and international venues and now serves as a reminder of those women who have gone before us, both for our freedom and in the world of quilting, and as a motivator for us today that We Can Do It!

Glossary

appliqué—the sewing or fusing of fabric pieces to a background fabric, creating a design

backing—the fabric that forms the bottom layer of a quilt sandwich

batting—the center layer of a quilt; is made of various materials (cotton, wool, polyester)

bias—the diagonal grain of fabric which is stretchier than the fabric straight-of-grain

binding—the fabric that finishes the edge of a quilt by encasing the raw edges of the quilt top, batting, and backing

block—a pieced or appliqued design unit of a quilt top

border—one (or more) pieced or single fabric strips sewn around the edges of a quilt top

cornerstone—a square placed at the corner of of sashing strips set between blocks in a quilt top

finished measurement—the size of a piece after it is sewn into a completed block; the size of a block in a completed quilt top

half-square triangle (HST)—a square quilt block unit constructed of two right-angle triangles

lock stitch-to make several small stitches or black stitches at the beginning and the end of a seam to secure the threads

LOF—length of fabric

miter—a 45-degree angle finish at a corner, either in the border of a block or quilt top or in the finishing of the binding

needle-turn appliqué—a method of applying fabric pieces to a background fabric where the edges of the piece are turned under with the point of a hand-held needle as the piece is sewn down

piecing—the sewing of fabric pieces or units to form a block

quarter-square triangle (QST)—a square quilt block unit constructed with four right-angle triangles

quilt sandwich—the quilt top, batting, and backing that make up the three layers of a quilt

quilt top—the pieced or appliqued layer of a quilt sandwich

quilting—the stitching that holds together the three layers of a quilt sandwich (quilt top, batting, and backing)

rotary ruler—an acrylic ruler designed specifically to be used with a rotary cutter

sashing—strips of fabric set between blocks in a quilt top

seam allowance—the amount of fabric between a stitching line and the edge; the quilting standard is ¼"

selvage—the heavily woven edges of fabric generally trimmed off and not used

straight-of-grain—the lengthwise or crosswise direction of the threads of a fabric

strip-set—one or more strips of fabric joined along the long edges from which units are cut

template—a paper or plastic pattern shape

unfinished measurement—the cut size of pieces in a block; the size of a unit or block before it is joined to other units or blocks

value—the intensity of color in a fabric, whether lighter or darker, as compared to the adjacent fabrics

WOF—width of fabric

Index

About the Authors
Leila Gardunia

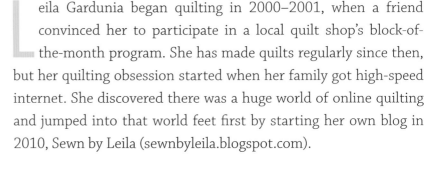

Leila Gardunia began quilting in 2000–2001, when a friend convinced her to participate in a local quilt shop's block-of-the-month program. She has made quilts regularly since then, but her quilting obsession started when her family got high-speed internet. She discovered there was a huge world of online quilting and jumped into that world feet first by starting her own blog in 2010, Sewn by Leila (sewnbyleila.blogspot.com).

In 2011, she started an online quilt-along, THE WE CAN DO IT! SKILL BUILDER SAMPLER as a way to stretch her quilting skills and teach others. The quilt-along made her realize that overcoming her fears was the hardest part of learning a new skill and that different quilting techniques were rarely as difficult as she imagined. This book is based on that quilt-along. Leila knows you can do it, too! She enjoys teaching children and adults basic garment sewing and quilting, as well as writing online tutorials. She is a contributor to the Moda Bake Shop and FaveQuilts.

Leila is a member of the Des Moines Modern Quilt Guild and serves as the Program Co-Chair. One of her quilts was shown at the first Modern Quilt Guild Show in 2013 and she has won awards for her quilting and sewing at the Iowa State Fair. She lives in small-town Iowa with her amazing husband, five wonderful daughters, and a cat.

Marlene Oddie

Marlene Oddie was a child when she made her first quilt. It was a hand appliquéd Sunbonnet Sue and Overall Sam which she hand tied with yarn. In 2001, her church started a quilting class which brought her back to the quilting world. She was soon asked to teach the class and organize the next year's projects. Later she took a long-arm machine class from Suzanne Young that furthered Marlene's passion for quilting. In 2009, after marrying Duncan Oddie, opportunity and circumstances allowed her to purchase her own long-arm quilting machine. It was then she began the full-time pursuit of her business, KISSed Quilts (Keeping it Simple and Stunning).

Marlene's designs have won ribbons locally, regionally, and internationally and have been selected for various publications. She writes regularly for the *Country Register* and was a finalist in the McCall's Quilt Design Star 2011. An Electric Quilt artist, she blogs with design and quilting tutorials at kissedquilts.blogspot.com and teaches wherever there is an interest. In 2013, she opened a quilting studio in Grand Coulee, Washington. Given Marlene's background as an industrial and systems engineer and a project manager in aerospace, her designs often come from engineering perspectives. She loves turning ideas into reality, especially a quilted item that can be cherished for years.

The Rosie the Riveter Poster

The printed fabric panel is available in a variety of sizes from Marlene's website, www.kissedquilts.com. It can be printed at www.spoonflower. com and quilt shops may sell prints to their customers. For more ideas, go to www.skillbuildersampler.com.

Other AQS Books

This is only a small selection of the books available from the American Quilter's Society. AQS books are known worldwide for timely topics, clear writing, beautiful color photos, and accurate illustrations and patterns. The following books are available from your local bookseller, quilt shop, or public library.

#1650. . . . . $22.95

#1420. . . . . $24.95

#1421. . . . . $24.95

#8664. . . . . $19.95

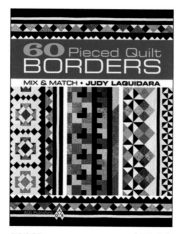

#8662. . . . . $26.95

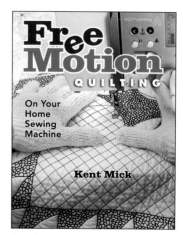

#1585. . . . . $12.95

#8770. . . . . $21.95

#8671. . . . . $24.95

#8663. . . . . $24.95